TEACHING *by* *the* SPIRIT

TEACHING *by* *the* SPIRIT

GENE R. COOK

DESERET
BOOK

SALT LAKE CITY, UTAH

Library of Congress Cataloging-in-Publication Data

Cook, Gene R.
  Teaching by the Spirit / Gene R. Cook
    p.   cm.
  Includes index.
  ISBN 1-57345-889-9 (HB)
    1. Church of Jesus Christ of Latter-day Saints—Education.
    2. Teachers—Religious life. 3. Christian education. 4. Holy spirit.
  I. Title

BX8610.C66 2000
268'.89332—dc21

00-050877

Printed in the United States of America   72082-6763

10   9   8   7   6   5   4   3   2   1

CONTENTS

ACKNOWLEDGMENTS

"Teaching by the Spirit." What an elevated and sacred doctrine! The very idea connotes an involvement on the part of the Lord to imbue a principle with his Spirit, and then by that same Spirit to convey it to the heart of another. What a profound process by which we learn truth.

My debt of gratitude to my Heavenly Father is greater than my ability to express. Through the years, he has taught me by the Spirit of the Lord the truth of the doctrines found in this book. There have been numerous times when the Spirit of the Lord has impressed a truth upon my heart and mind, and I knew that I had been directly taught by the Spirit. There have been times when I have sat in a meeting and tried purposefully to humble myself that I might be open to learning by the Spirit. A confirmation has come as the Lord taught me something or reconfirmed or expanded the truth to me. What a glorious experience!

The Lord has also often utilized others to teach me by the Spirit. I am deeply indebted to the General Authorities of the Church, especially the prophets, seers, and revelators of this dispensation with whom I have had the privilege of serving through the years. They have consistently employed these sacred principles to teach the doctrines of the Lord, conveying them with power to the hearts of the children of men.

There are others, as well, whom the Lord has inspired to teach and cause me to learn by the Spirit, mainly my parents, my wife, my children, good teachers throughout the Church, and even good people not of our faith. All these the Lord has touched, and the Spirit has taught me through them. To all of these, I am indebted for having been the beneficiary of their *teaching by the Spirit.*

A special thanks goes to Brother Jay A. Parry, who has provided valued assistance in the editing and preparation of the manuscript for printing. Jay has a gift for being able to say things succinctly and with meaning and feeling. For that, I am most thankful. He has been most valuable in reading the manuscript with new eyes and being able to make insightful suggestions to improve the content. He is an excellent editor.

Lastly, I would like to say that this book is not in any way an official publication of The Church of Jesus Christ of Latter-day Saints. Any shortcomings, omissions, or deficiencies are clearly mine as the one solely responsible for the material in this book.

CHAPTER 1

WHO IS A TEACHER?

When I was growing up I had a number of fine teachers in the Church. But often others teach us besides those who are called to do so. An example that illustrates this principle is how I came to obtain my own testimony.

My older brother had always been an inspiration to me. One evening when he was about seventeen, he came home from a Church youth meeting and announced to me that his teacher had told him to gain his own testimony and not to rely on those of others. He said—almost prophetically—"I'm going to gain that personal witness and testimony, no matter how long it takes or what the cost. I will pay the price to know."

He then began fasting, praying, and studying the Book of Mormon. One morning a short time later, he was stricken by paralysis. He could not move his body, and his right side was in terrible pain. He was barely able to whisper to my father that he wanted a blessing. As soon as the blessing was completed, my brother was miraculously healed. He uncoiled his tense body, straightened up, and was free of pain.

When he was later examined by a doctor, the diagnosis was that he had had what appeared to be a ruptured appendix, but no trace of damaged tissue was found in his body. Later, my brother told me of his feelings about being healed, and he told me that he knew the Church was true. However, he said a spiritual witness of the Book of Mormon had come before the healing. He told me how he had studied the book and prayed over every page. He bore his testimony to me. I was very touched by this experience, and I said in my heart, "If the Lord will answer my brother, he will also answer me."

Thus at age twelve I began to read the Book of Mormon. I, too, received a personal confirmation of the truthfulness of the gospel. I knew then and have never doubted since that the Book of Mormon is the word of God and that the gospel is true.

It is now clear to me that my brother's testimony reached my heart and caused me to desire the same thing he had. Though he was just a teenager himself, my brother was a powerful teacher in my life.

ALL ARE TEACHERS

Who is a teacher? We all are! Think about the many roles in our lives that involve teaching: father, mother, caring brother or sister, home teacher, visiting teacher, ward or stake leader, teacher in a Church class, speaker in a meeting, missionary, neighbor, and so on. As Elder Jeffrey R. Holland said, "In this Church it is virtually impossible to find anyone who is *not* a guide of one kind or another to his or her fellow members of the flock" ("'A Teacher Come from God,'"*Ensign,* May 1998, 25).

The Church has spent much time and many resources to teach us how to be good teachers. All members are encouraged to take the Teaching the Gospel course, a twelve-week series of lessons that give us a basic understanding of how to teach better. Lessons include such topics as loving those you teach, teaching by the Spirit, teaching the doctrine of the kingdom, the role of the learner, and effective methods of teaching. In addition, all leaders and teachers are invited to attend a quarterly teacher improvement meeting designed to upgrade the level of teaching in the wards, branches, and homes of the Church.

Resources for this training are also wonderful resources for personal reading and review: *Teaching, No Greater Call: A Resource Guide for Gospel Teaching;* and "Gospel Teaching and Leadership," Section 16 of the *Church Handbook of Instructions, Book 2: Priesthood and Auxiliary Leaders,* which is to be distributed to all teachers and leaders in the Church. (Both are published by the Church and are available in Church distribution centers.)

Elder Boyd K. Packer underscored the idea that we are all teachers, even as we serve in other roles and callings: "The prophet is a teacher; his counselors are teachers; the General Authorities are teachers. Stake presidents and mission presidents are teachers; high councilors and quorum presidents are teachers; bishops are teachers; and so through all of the organizations of the Church. The Church moves forward sustained by the power of the teaching that is accomplished" (*Teach Ye Diligently,* rev. ed. [Salt Lake City: Deseret Book Co., 1991], 3–4).

Elder Holland continues: "To teach effectively and to feel you are succeeding is demanding work indeed. But it is worth it. We can receive 'no greater call.' (*Teaching—No Greater Call* [resource materials for teacher improvement, 1978]; see also Spencer W. Kimball, "No Greater Call," Sunday School Conference, 1 Oct. 1967.) Surely the opportunity to magnify that call exists everywhere. The need for it is everlasting. Fathers, mothers, siblings, friends, missionaries, home and visiting teachers, priesthood and auxiliary leaders, classroom instructors—each is, in his or her own way, 'come from God' for our schooling and our salvation. . . .

"For each of us to 'come unto Christ' (D&C 20:59), to keep His commandments and follow His example back to the Father is surely the highest and holiest purpose of human existence. To help others do that as well—to teach, persuade, and prayerfully lead them to walk that path of redemption also—surely that must be the second most significant task in our lives. Perhaps that is why President David O. McKay once said, 'No

greater responsibility can rest upon any man [or woman], than
to be a teacher of God's children' (in Conference Report, Oct.
1916, 57)" ("'A Teacher Come from God,'" *Ensign*, May 1998,
25).

President Gordon B. Hinckley has said, "Effective teaching
is the very essence of leadership in the Church. Eternal life will
come only as men and women are taught with such effective-
ness that they change and discipline their lives. They cannot be
coerced into righteousness or into heaven. They must be led,
and that means teaching" ("How to Be a Teacher When Your
Role as a Leader Requires You to Teach," General Authority
Priesthood Board Meeting, 5 Feb. 1969).

Since we all are teachers, and since teaching is so important, then it makes sense that we would seek to learn to do our
teaching in the Lord's way. And what is the Lord's way? He has
admonished us to do our teaching by the power of his Spirit.
As we do, we will lift and bless others as we can in no other
way.

THE EXAMPLE OF A WONDERFUL GRANDMOTHER

It's probably clear to all of us that we should seek to teach
powerful and Spirit-filled lessons in Gospel Doctrine class. But,
since we all are teachers, we should seek to teach such lessons
in more obscure settings as well, as we seek to reach and bless
those we love and work with. Someone who influenced me in a
mighty way by teaching by the Spirit was my Grandma Elsie
Hanna Cook. I share her example here because it can serve as
a model for us all.

My grandmother Cook was a great woman, a woman of
much faith. Some of my earliest memories about spiritual
things are intertwined with memories of her. When our family
was living in Boise, Idaho, my parents were only partly active
in the Church. But Grandma Cook went to Church faithfully,

and she tried to make sure that her two oldest Cook grandsons, Ron and me, went to Church with her. Many times we walked with her from our home to the Church, which was a mile or two away.

When I was about ten years old we moved to Mesa, Arizona, and Grandma Cook moved with us. While I was a paperboy she subscribed to the *Phoenix Gazette.* I suspect her subscription had more to do with the delivery boy than with her desire to read the paper. Each day when I stopped by with the paper, she would have a cupcake or a cookie waiting for me. In addition, she would often say, "Gene, if you have just a minute you can spare from delivering papers, come in and let's have a prayer. I'm not feeling very well today."

We would go in by her big brass bed and kneel together and pray. When she offered the prayer, she would always pray for me, asking the Lord to strengthen and bless me in the gospel. Many times she would ask me to say the prayer, which I did. I found as the weeks went by and we prayed together, the love we had for each other was being greatly strengthened.

Grandma Cook seemed to be one who always turned to the Lord first when she had a problem. And she was always quick to recognize the hand of the Lord in blessing her life. She seemed to cause me to be more aware of his existence than any other person I'm aware of, and she taught me as much as anyone else about how involved he was in everything. Even in little things she would say, "Look how the Lord has blessed us, Gene. Look how the Lord has blessed you. Look what the Lord has done in softening so-and-so's heart. Look how the Lord is helping my granddaughter or my grandson."

One of Grandma's greatest attributes was her ability to have faith in other people. She worked on a nonmember who lived across the street, helping him to finally quit smoking. She worked on encouraging a widow across the street. She worked on a nonmember neighbor lady who was married to a member who was totally inactive. The neighbor lady joined the Church; her husband returned to activity; and in time he became the bishop of his ward. Grandma talked to anyone and everyone about the gospel, bearing testimony of its truthfulness, and showing great faith in the Lord by her example.

Above all, she touched others with the deep love in her heart, and she taught them by the Spirit.

Teaching by the Spirit: Being Edified Together

> Wherefore, he that preacheth and he that receiveth, understand one another, and both are edified and rejoice together. (D&C 50:22.)

If someone in a congregation is truly listening by the Spirit and someone else is speaking by the Spirit, a real connection will result. But even if someone is *speaking* by the Spirit, that connection will not be there unless those in the meeting are *listening* by the Spirit.

Think of this analogy: What if I were to speak to you in Spanish? What if I were to say, "*¿Cuantos de ustedes me entienden? Si me entienden levanten por favor su mano.*" I have performed this experiment in a congregation, asking those who understand my Spanish to raise their hands. Out of a large group of listeners, only three raised their hands. I jokingly asked, "Where are the rest of you?" (The translation of the above Spanish sentences is "How many of you understand me? If you understand me, please raise your hand.")

Isn't that amazing? I speak another language, and all of a sudden I am understood by only those who know the language.

Learning and teaching by the Spirit are somewhat like that. If we are not praying in a meeting to be humble in our own hearts and to be able to truly listen by the Spirit of the Lord, we'll get about as much out of it as we would when trying to understand another language—Spanish or Swahili—that we have not learned. We may hear the words with our ears, but we need the Spirit to really understand the message with our hearts.

President Marion G. Romney once related this experience: He had been speaking to a large group of missionaries, and after he finished his talk he followed a group out into the hallway where he overheard two missionaries speaking. One of them said, "This is absolutely the most boring meeting I've ever attended in my whole life. When do we get lunch?" When his companion didn't answer, the missionary turned to him and saw that the companion had tears running down his cheeks. "This is absolutely the best meeting I've ever attended in my whole life," that companion said.

We can't help but wonder: How can it be that they were both in the same meeting? Or were they? They heard the same things. But while one of them was anxious about lunch, the other learned by the Spirit of the Lord something that may have changed his entire life. I'm convinced that when we teach by the Spirit and listen by the Spirit, changes occur in people's hearts. They understand in their minds that which is being taught, they feel it in their hearts, and then they go and act. Because they feel the witness of the Spirit, their lives are filled with determination, desire, and obedience.

Where to Teach by the Spirit

I believe the Lord would have his Sunday School and Primary teachers all teach their lessons as they are guided and strengthened by the Spirit. I believe it is vital that Church leaders teach by the Spirit in interviews and council meetings, that sacrament meeting speakers teach by the Spirit when they talk, and that home teachers and visiting teachers teach by the Spirit when they visit. But so also should parents, and brothers and sisters, and all the Grandma Cooks in the world. When our teaching and listening come by the Spirit, as we will explain in subsequent chapters, real learning occurs and a change of heart comes.

This book will give some suggestions to making that happen, in love and with power, "at all times and in all things, and in all places" (Mosiah 18:9).

QUESTIONS TO PONDER

1. What are some of the roles in your life in which you could see yourself as a teacher?

_____

_____

_____

2. Can you think of some individuals in your life who were not teachers, but still had a great teaching influence on you? What did they do to make a difference in your life?

_____

_____

_____

3. Are there some settings in your life where you are not formally a teacher but where you could have a greater impact in leading people to Christ?

_____

_____

_____

CHAPTER 2

THE ROLE OF THE
SPIRIT IN TEACHING

Several years ago I had the opportunity to tour one of our South American missions under the direction of the mission president. (I'll call him President Jones.) This particular mission had been having tremendous success in terms of baptisms, with some five hundred or six hundred per month. The president was anxious to progress and do even better.

When I had a preliminary visit with President Jones a few months earlier, I learned that he was a very positive individual. He had read quite a number of positive-thinking books and was particularly focusing on that kind of material with his missionaries. At that time I confirmed that one can indeed get results by using the positive-thinking techniques of the world. But I tried to teach him that those approaches must be totally founded in spiritual concepts, or the experience will not develop the long-term faith of the missionary. I think he only partially understood what I was trying to say.

When we were ready to begin the tour, I asked him if he would be willing for us to teach the missionaries that it was time to move up another level in our approach. We were going to replace the teachings of the positive-thinking gurus with the teachings of the Lord as found in the scriptures, thus basing our work on faith in the Lord Jesus Christ and not on the philosophies of men, even if they contain truths. I suggested that instead of following the approach of a man (even though he may be a good and wise man), we should follow the counsel of the Lord: to teach by the Spirit. He indicated that he was willing, but he wasn't sure we could have success with that approach.

I had him write on a piece of paper the five major premises or principles taught by the author of his favorite positive-thinking book. Some of the concepts that these men have developed are true because they learned them from the Lord, even if they aren't aware of it. However, the Lord speaks through his prophets in a deeper and truer sense than man can speak. Thus, I wanted us to see what the scriptures taught about each of the principles President Jones had been using.

I think he had doubts about whether or not these principles could be effectively illustrated from the scriptures. We looked at the first principle, which was having a healthy self-image, and we talked about Moses, Saul, and Joseph Smith. We took the second concept, about the power of faith, and illustrated it from the scriptures. Before we had spent much time on it, he realized that the scriptures teach truth much more powerfully than man can ever teach it.

As we proceeded with the conferences, President Jones indicated to all of the missionaries that it was time for a change. I underscored the same idea in my own teaching, never mentioning the particular author the mission president had emphasized but testifying of the power of the Lord and of the need for faith in the Lord Jesus Christ. The entire tour was a powerful experience for both of us, and it gave President Jones a new vision. When he reported to me some time later, he said that the mission's baptisms had not gone down—and the missionaries seemed to be increasing in their spirituality.

At the conclusion of the tour, Sister Jones, who is very learned in religious study, said, "I've never been more humbled in all my life. I feel like a failure. I need to start all over again and teach true spiritual things, not the academic spiritual things." I think she began to sense more than ever the great power of the Lord. And she seemed to be feeling that, at least in one sense, they had lost much in the previous 2 1/2 years by not using that power more effectively.

If missionaries want to read such positive-thinking authors when they get home, they may receive some helpful insights. But the Spirit of the Lord is the true source of power in our lives. It is that source that we should seek in our teaching, our learning, and our practice of the gospel from day to day.

Once I attended a Gospel Doctrine class that seemed to be the opposite of that which the Lord describes. The teacher brought in a stack of books with him to the class, and referred to many of them as he taught—but he didn't use even one scripture. The class seemed to be *centered* on the teacher. Some doctrine was presented, but it was definitely not being taught by the Spirit.

As the lesson proceeded I sat and agonized, because I could see and feel some real needs in the hearts of at least four people who sat near me. I sensed they were carrying real burdens. They had come to the class to be refreshed and to have the Spirit touch their hearts; they had come seeking some answers to life's problems. But the teacher was too busy conveying information to recognize those spiritual needs. Unfortunately, we sometimes get in the mode of "unloading" information rather than seeking to bless and change hearts.

When we get ourselves into a pattern of teaching or learning that does not involve the Spirit, it can be difficult to get out. I think sometimes of this little poem:

> The sermon ended,
> The priest descended.
> Delighted were they,
> But preferred the old way.

We all have a tendency to stick with "the old way." But if we have not truly been teaching by the Spirit, I would challenge each of us to resolve to change now, as the mission president in this example humbly did. That is the path of blessing both for ourselves and for those we teach.

"UNTO WHAT WERE YE ORDAINED?"

The Lord has spoken through his latter-day prophets to tell us how he would have us teach: "Wherefore, I the Lord ask you this question—unto what were ye ordained?" When we think of our callings as teacher, priesthood leader, or parent, what were we ordained to do? The Lord gives the answer: "To preach my gospel by the Spirit, even the Comforter which was sent forth to teach the truth" (D&C 50:13–14).

Who will assist us in our efforts to preach the gospel? The Spirit. And who was sent forth to actually do the teaching? The Comforter. The Lord is the One who knows the needs of those being taught. He is the One who can impress someone's heart and cause him or her to change. We are instruments, helpers—not the primary teacher. *The major role of a teacher is to prepare the way so that the people will have a spiritual experience with the Lord.*

We must make sure we don't begin to think we are the "true teacher." That is a serious mistake. Yes, we are part of the process. But ultimately all true gospel teaching is done by the Holy Ghost. He is the teacher, not us. We must be careful not to get in the way.

Doctrine and Covenants 50 continues:

> Verily I say unto you, he that is ordained of me and sent forth to preach the word of truth by the Comforter, in the Spirit of truth, doth he preach *it* by the Spirit of truth or some other way? And if it be by some other way it is not of God. (D&C 50:17–18; emphasis added.)

What is the *it* in that sentence? The word of truth. We must teach the word of truth by the Spirit, and if we teach the word of truth some other way, even if it is true, it is not of God. Some teachers fall into a trap of thinking that just because they've taught truth, their lesson was acceptable. But the Lord says that if you do not preach the truth with the Spirit, what you are doing is not of God.

This truth also applies to learning:

> And again, he that receiveth the word of truth, doth he receive it by the Spirit of truth or some other way? If it be some other way it is not of God. (D&C 50:19–20.)

The Spirit is a key element in both teaching and learning—and if the Spirit is not present, the sharing even of truth is not of God.

Other scriptures emphasize this role of the Spirit:

> The elders, priests and teachers of this church shall teach the principles of my gospel . . . *as they shall be directed by the Spirit.* And the Spirit shall be given unto you by the prayer of faith; and *if ye receive not the Spirit ye shall not teach.* (D&C 42:12–14; emphasis added.)

> But the Comforter, which is the Holy Ghost, whom the Father will send in my name, *he shall teach you all things,* and bring all things to your remembrance, whatsoever I have said unto you. (John 14:26; emphasis added.)

> Let my [servants] . . . proclaim the things which I have commanded them—Calling on the name of the Lord for the Comforter, *which shall teach them all things* that are expedient for them. (D&C 75:9–10; emphasis added.)

> I will send upon him the Comforter, *which shall teach him the truth* and the way whither he shall go. (D&C 79:2; emphasis added.)

And by the power of the Holy Ghost *ye may know the truth of all things.* (Moroni 10:5; emphasis added.)

If any of you lack wisdom, let him ask *of God.* (James 1:5; emphasis added.)

Joseph Fielding Smith explained why the Spirit is such a key element in teaching: "The Spirit of God speaking to the spirit of man has power to impart truth with greater effect and understanding than the truth can be imparted by personal contact even with heavenly beings. Through the Holy Ghost the truth is woven into the very fibre and sinews of the body so that it cannot be forgotten" (*Doctrines of Salvation,* comp. Bruce R. McConkie, 3 vols. [Salt Lake City: Bookcraft, 1954–56], 1:47–48).

President Spencer W. Kimball once encouraged us: "I fear that all too often many of our members come to church, sit through a class or a meeting, and they then return home having been largely [uninspired]. It is especially unfortunate when this happens at a time . . . of stress, temptation, or crisis [in their lives]. *We all need to be touched and nurtured by the Spirit, and effective teaching is one of the most important ways this can happen*" (*Teachings of Spencer W. Kimball,* ed. Edward L. Kimball [Salt Lake City: Bookcraft, 1982], 524; emphasis added).

THE TEACHER'S TRUE ROLE

When we understand correctly, then, we see that our role is to prepare ourselves to be worthy, to prepare the environment, and to present certain material in a teaching setting—and then the Holy Ghost will do the teaching. Certainly we can learn things from other people; another man or woman can teach us things we need to know. But if we want permanent change, the Holy Ghost must be involved.

This concept of the role of the Spirit in teaching is reflected in the Church's current approach to lesson manuals. In years past, the Church provided long and detailed lesson plans for each Sunday class that was taught. Now, the many pages per lesson have been cut down to just a few.

After we had reduced the Gospel Doctrine manuals to many fewer pages (I was on the committee that helped determine the new approach), a friend said to me, "Elder Cook, I can't believe that you would agree to that. You teach with many stories and illustrations, but now you've stripped them all out of the manual." I responded by saying, "For years we have found or created great stories about tithing or answers to prayer and have distributed them all over the world. But think about it: right in your own class you've got forty or fifty people who have had experience with that principle just in the last week. They could stand up and bear witness of how the Lord has changed their life in the last week, and do it with the Spirit."

Teachers need to learn how to draw stories and experiences out of the people so that the Spirit of the Lord can teach both the teacher and the learner. Then both will be "edified and rejoice together" (D&C 50:22).

The most important thing a teacher can do is to help the student feel the Spirit of the Lord. If the Spirit is there, true teaching and true learning will take place, and lives will begin to be changed.

I become a little worried sometimes that many teachers are not concerned enough about trying to have the Spirit of the Lord with them *all the time* while they are teaching. Again, if you don't, you shall not teach—at least not the Lord's way.

TRUSTING THE SPIRIT TO TEACH

I suspect we sometimes think that if we don't convey all the information we have on a subject, those we teach won't learn what they need to know. But I would suggest a different perspective. As we develop greater trust in the Lord, we will know that if we can bring the Spirit into a teaching situation, that Spirit will help the other person to learn and know what is most essential.

I am familiar with a true story that illustrates this. Once President Spencer W. Kimball telephoned a man (I'll call him Brother Smith) and told him that the Lord wanted him to serve as a temple president. Brother Smith was stunned, feeling both unworthy and unprepared. But President Kimball assured him that the call had indeed been confirmed by the Lord and that it was right. "I'm going to be visiting your city next month," President Kimball said. "I'd like to meet with you at the temple to set you apart and bestow on you the sealing power."

President Kimball met with Brother Smith at the appointed time. As was his custom, President Kimball threw his arms around Brother Smith and loved him and told him that the Lord would help him and bless him. They visited for a few minutes; then President Kimball placed his hands on Brother Smith's head and set him apart as a temple president and gave him the sealing power. When he was finished, President Kimball said, "Brother Smith, the Lord will bless you." And President Kimball turned and started to leave.

Brother Smith said, "But President, I don't know anything about being a temple president. What shall I do?" President Kimball simply said, "Well, the Lord will bless you, my friend," and he walked down the corridor of the temple.

Brother Smith followed him. "Wait, President, wait! I've never been anything but a temple patron. What if the cafeteria workers quit or the temple veil rips? What will I do?"

"Well, just call the Temple Department; they'll help you on things like that." President Kimball walked out into the parking lot and began to get into his car. Brother Smith said, almost begging, "President, please, won't you give me one piece of counsel?" And President Kimball turned and, with a big smile and a sparkle in his eye, said, "Well, President Smith, it wouldn't hurt you to lose about thirty pounds." He again expressed his love to him, got into his car, and drove off.

Was President Kimball being insensitive to the man's need? No, he wanted to teach the man to turn to the Lord, where he would be taught by the Spirit. President Kimball was doing the best thing any teacher can do: turning the learning to the Master Teacher himself.

Let me add to that story a personal experience. When I was called to be a mission president I had been a General Authority for a year already. Shortly before we were to leave President Kimball called and said, "Elder Cook, we really need to set you apart as a mission president. Why don't you come by my office and bring your wife and your children, if you like?" We took our two oldest boys, who were maybe six or seven at the time, and went to President Kimball's office. On the way I said to my wife, "Here, we're going to serve among the Lamanites. Who in all the world knows more about the Lamanites than President Kimball? Nobody does. What a unique opportunity. After he sets me apart, I'll ask him for a little counsel." (I didn't know about Brother Smith's experience at the time!)

President Kimball set me apart, loved our family, and committed my wife and the children in their roles in our calling. As things were winding down, I said, "Well, President, as you know we're called to serve in Uruguay and Paraguay. We'd be delighted if you had any counsel you could give us about serving among the Lamanites." I thought it was a good request. President Kimball paused and then said, "Well, let's see now, Gene, do you hold the Melchizedek Priesthood?" I knew I was in trouble then. I had to say, "Yes." "And you've been set apart as a General Authority, and as a mission president now?" "Yes." Then he said, "Adios." And that was it. We left without a word of instruction.

Why did President Kimball send a mission president off to

a foreign land without any special instruction? Why did he call a temple president without giving him any counsel? Here are at least two reasons: First, he knew that we would be instructed through the proper channels. (President Kimball *did* believe in training.) Second, he knew that the Lord would give us the guidance we needed, through his Spirit. President Kimball set the stage by his expressions of love and by his inspired words in setting us apart. And then he turned us over to the Lord and trusted the Spirit to continue our instruction.

TURN THE LISTENER TO THE LORD

President Kimball teaches another valuable lesson in these stories. One of the best things the teacher can do is to turn his listener to the Lord. Elder Richard G. Scott suggested this principle when he said, "If you accomplish nothing else in your relationship with your students than to help them recognize and follow the promptings of the Spirit, you will bless their lives immeasurably and eternally" (*Helping Others to Be Spiritually Led*, address to religious educators, 11 Aug. 1998, 3).

President Kimball truly believed that Church callings come from the Lord. And since the Lord had called the temple president and mission president in those stories, He also had an interest in helping them to become prepared and qualified for their service.

Certainly as the President of the Church, President Kimball could have kept the temple president there for an hour and told him all he knew about temple work. President Kimball could have kept him there for a day or a week. He could have done the same with me in giving me instruction about the Lamanites when I was called as a mission president. So why didn't he? Because his approach taught us to turn to the Lord for help and instruction.

That is one of the greatest gifts a teacher can give to his or her students—to turn them to the Lord for answers. President Kimball could have given us good advice. But instead he gave us something far greater—the gift of seeking and yearning for a closer relationship with the Lord.

These stories also teach us that we should be careful not to answer every question that is put to us as teachers. Sometimes we can perform a much greater service by choosing not to answer, by inviting students to think things through themselves, to send them back to the Lord for instructions. This counsel applies to children as well as to adults. When we are asked a tough question, perhaps the answer might be, "Well, what do you think, John?" Or, "John, why don't you carefully pray about that and let's talk about it tomorrow. Let me know what you think the Lord says you ought to do."

Nephi did that, teaching his brothers principles that he hoped would cause them to want to turn to the Lord. As we read in 1 Nephi:

> For he truly spake many great things unto them, which were hard to be understood, save a man should inquire of the Lord; and they being hard in their hearts, therefore they did not look unto the Lord as they ought. (1 Nephi 15:3.)

Nephi "was grieved" (1 Nephi 15:4) because his brothers would not ask of the Lord. They did not want to be taught by the Spirit. When they came to him and said they could not understand some of his teachings, he asked them pointedly, "Have ye inquired of the Lord?" (1 Nephi 15:8). That is a good question for us to ask of ourselves, often—and it is a question we should seek to guide others to ask as well, that they may more thoroughly be taught by the Spirit of the Lord.

FOLLOWING JESUS, THE MODEL TEACHER

When we read the gospels, it is clear that Jesus was a master teacher. In fact, he was *the* master teacher. As Elder Bruce R. McConkie wrote, he was "the greatest Teacher ever to grace the earth, . . . the Master Teacher whose message and methods would set the perfect standard for all apostles, all prophets, all preachers of righteousness, all teachers, of all ages" (*The Promised Messiah* [Salt Lake City: Deseret Book Co., 1978], 510).

As the master teacher, Jesus always knew exactly what to say, how to say it, and when. We can have the same blessing if we truly seek and follow the Spirit in our lives and in our teaching.

On one occasion when Jesus was teaching, one of his listeners stood and asked, "Master, what shall I do to inherit eternal life?"

Rather than answer the man directly, Jesus responded with another question: "What is written in the law? how readest thou?"

The man answered by saying, "Thou shalt love the Lord thy God with all thy heart, and with all thy soul, and with all thy strength, and with all thy mind; and thy neighbour as thyself."

"Thou hast answered right," Jesus said; "this do, and thou shalt live."

But the man was not satisfied and questioned further, asking, "Who is my neighbour?"

Jesus answered the man's second question by telling him a short story with a setting and circumstance that the man would recognize:

> A certain man went down from Jerusalem to Jericho, and fell among thieves, which stripped him of his raiment, and wounded him, and departed, leaving him half dead. And by chance there came down a certain priest

that way: and when he saw him, he passed by on the other side. And likewise a Levite, when he was at the place, came and looked on him, and passed by on the other side. But a certain Samaritan, as he journeyed, came where he was: and when he saw him, he had compassion on him, and went to him, and bound up his wounds, pouring in oil and wine, and set him on his own beast, and brought him to an inn, and took care of him. And on the morrow when he departed, he took out two pence, and gave them to the host, and said unto him, Take care of him; and whatsoever thou spendest more, when I come again, I will repay thee.

After telling the parable, Jesus asked another question: "Which now of these three, thinkest thou, was neighbour unto him that fell among the thieves?" The questioner said, "He that shewed mercy on him." Then Jesus said, "Go, and do thou likewise" (Luke 10:25–37).

Without question and beyond all comparison, Jesus was the greatest teacher who ever lived. We can improve our own teaching of gospel truths as we follow the perfect pattern shown in Jesus' teaching.

Jesus Taught from the Scriptures

After Jesus had fasted forty days and forty nights in the wilderness,

> the tempter came to him [and] said, If thou be the Son of God, command that these stones be made bread. But he answered and said, *It is written*, Man shall not live by bread alone, but by every word that proceedeth out of the mouth of God.
>
> Then the devil taketh him up into the holy city, and setteth him on a pinnacle of the temple, and saith unto him, If thou be the Son of God, cast thyself down: for it is written, He shall give his angels charge concerning thee:

and in their hands they shall bear thee up, lest at any time thou dash thy foot against a stone. Jesus said unto him, *It is written again,* Thou shalt not tempt the Lord thy God.

Again, the devil taketh him up into an exceeding high mountain, and sheweth him all the kingdoms of the world, and the glory of them; and saith unto him, All these things will I give thee, if thou wilt fall down and worship me. Then saith Jesus unto him, Get thee hence, Satan: for *it is written,* Thou shalt worship the Lord thy God, and him only shalt thou serve. (Matthew 4:3–10; emphasis added.)

In each instance of dealing with Satan's challenges Jesus responded by quoting the scriptures. Jesus used the same approach on other occasions. For example, once Jesus' disciples plucked some ears of corn as they walked through a field on the Sabbath. The Pharisees interpreted that as a violation of the law of Moses.

And the Pharisees said unto him, Behold, why do [the disciples] on the sabbath day that which is not lawful? And he said unto them, *Have ye never read what David did,* when he had need, and was an hungred, he, and they that were with him? How he went into the house of God in the days of Abiathar the high priest, and did eat the shewbread, which is not lawful to eat but for the priests, and gave also to them which were with him? And he said unto them, The sabbath was made for man, and not man for the sabbath: Therefore the Son of man is Lord also of the sabbath. (Mark 2:24–28; emphasis added.)

JESUS TAUGHT BY ASKING QUESTIONS

As we saw above, Jesus was a master at teaching by asking questions. Here are a few additional examples:

And, behold, there was a man which had his hand withered. And they asked him, saying, Is it lawful to heal on the sabbath days? that they might accuse him. And he said unto them, *What man shall there be among you, that shall have one sheep, and if it fall into a pit on the sabbath day, will he not lay hold on it, and lift it out? How much then is a man better than a sheep?* Wherefore it is lawful to do well on the sabbath days. Then saith he to the man, Stretch forth thine hand. And he stretched it forth; and it was restored whole, like as the other. (Matthew 12:10–13 emphasis added.)

Then came to Jesus scribes and Pharisees, which were of Jerusalem, saying, Why do thy disciples transgress the tradition of the elders? for they wash not their hands when they eat bread. But he answered and said unto them, *Why do ye also transgress the commandment of God by your tradition?* For God commanded, saying, Honour thy father and mother: and, He that curseth father or mother, let him die the death. But ye say, Whosoever shall say to his father or his mother, It is a gift, by whatsoever thou mightest be profited by me; and honour not his father or his mother, he shall be free. Thus have ye made the commandment of God of none effect by your tradition. (Matthew 15:1–6; emphasis added.)

And he called the multitude, and said unto them, Hear, and understand: Not that which goeth into the mouth defileth a man; but that which cometh out of the mouth, this defileth a man. Then came his disciples, and said unto him, Knowest thou that the Pharisees were offended, after they heard this saying? But he answered and said, Every plant, which my heavenly Father hath not planted, shall be rooted up. Let them alone: they be blind leaders of the blind. And if the blind lead the blind, both shall fall into the ditch.

Then answered Peter and said unto him, Declare unto us this parable. And Jesus said, *Are ye also yet without understanding? Do not ye yet understand, that whatsoever enentereth in at the mouth goeth into the belly, and is cast out into the draught?* But those things which proceed out of the mouth come forth from the heart; and they defile the man. For out of the heart proceed evil thoughts, murders, adulteries, fornications, thefts, false witness, blasphemies: These are the things which defile a man: but to eat with unwashen hands defileth not a man. (Matthew 15:10–20; emphasis added.)

For the Son of man is come to save that which was lost. *How think ye? if a man have an hundred sheep, and one of them be gone astray, doth he not leave the ninety and nine, and goeth into the mountains, and seeketh that which is gone astray?* And if so be that he find it, verily I say unto you, he rejoiceth more of that sheep, than of the ninety and nine which went not astray. Even so it is not the will of your Father which is in heaven, that one of these little ones should perish. (Matthew 18:11–14; emphasis added.)

And when he was come into the temple, the chief priests and the elders of the people came unto him as he was teaching, and said, By what authority doest thou these things? and who gave thee this authority? And Jesus answered and said unto them, I also will ask you one thing, which if ye tell me, I in like wise will tell you by what authority I do these things. *The baptism of John, whence was it? from heaven, or of men?* And they reasoned with themselves, saying, If we shall say, From heaven; he will say unto us, Why did ye not then believe him? But if we shall say, Of men; we fear the people; for all hold John as a prophet. And they answered Jesus, and said, We cannot tell. And he said unto them, Neither tell I you by what authority I do these things. (Matthew 21:23–27; emphasis added.)

JESUS TAUGHT BY USING ANALOGIES

By reviewing the thirteenth chapter of Matthew alone we can see several excellent examples of Jesus teaching by use of analogies:

> Another parable put he forth unto them, saying, The kingdom of heaven is *like to a grain of mustard seed,* which a man took, and sowed in his field: which indeed is the least of all seeds: but when it is grown, it is the greatest among herbs, and becometh a tree, so that the birds of the air come and lodge in the branches thereof.
>
> Another parable spake he unto them; The kingdom of heaven is *like unto leaven,* which a woman took, and hid in three measures of meal, till the whole was leavened. . . .
>
> Again, the kingdom of heaven is *like unto treasure hid in a field;* the which when a man hath found, he hideth, and for joy thereof goeth and selleth all that he hath, and buyeth that field.
>
> Again, the kingdom of heaven is *like unto a merchant man, seeking goodly pearls:* who, when he had found one pearl of great price, went and sold all that he had, and bought it.
>
> Again, the kingdom of heaven is *like unto a net,* that was cast into the sea, and gathered of every kind: which, when it was full, they drew to shore, and sat down, and gathered the good into vessels, but cast the bad away. So shall it be at the end of the world: the angels shall come forth, and sever the wicked from among the just. . . .
>
> Then said he unto them, Therefore every scribe which is instructed unto the kingdom of heaven is *like unto a man that is an householder,* which bringeth forth out of his treasure things new and old. (Matthew 13:31–33, 44–49, 52; emphasis added.)

JESUS TAUGHT BY USING REASON

The Savior was inspired in using the force of his intellect in his teaching. For instance, the Pharisees once accused Jesus of casting out devils by the power of Satan, saying,

> This fellow doth not cast out devils, but by Beelzebub the prince of the devils. And Jesus knew their thoughts, and said unto them, *Every kingdom divided against itself is brought to desolation; and every city or house divided against itself shall not stand: and if Satan cast out Satan, he is divided against himself; how shall then his kingdom stand?* And if I by Beelzebub cast out devils, by whom do your children cast them out? therefore they shall be your judges. But if I cast out devils by the Spirit of God, then the kingdom of God is come unto you. Or else how can one enter into a strong man's house, and spoil his goods, except he first bind the strong man? and then he will spoil his house. (Matthew 12:24–29; emphasis added.)

> And the scribes and the Pharisees began to reason, saying, Who is this which speaketh blasphemies? Who can forgive sins, but God alone? But when Jesus perceived their thoughts, he answering said unto them, *What reason ye in your hearts? Whether is easier, to say, Thy sins be forgiven thee; or to say, Rise up and walk? But that ye may know that the Son of man hath power upon earth to forgive sins, (he said unto the sick of the palsy,) I say unto thee, Arise,* and take up thy couch, and go into thine house. And immediately he rose up before them, and took up that whereon he lay, and departed to his own house, glorifying God. And they were all amazed, and they glorified God, and were filled with fear, saying, We have seen strange things to day. (Luke 5:21–26; emphasis added.)

JESUS TAUGHT BY USING PARABLES

Parables are one of the most commonly known teaching methods used by our Lord in mortality:

And *he spake many things unto them in parables,* saying, Behold, a sower went forth to sow; and when he sowed, some seeds fell by the way side, and the fowls came and devoured them up: some fell upon stony places, where they had not much earth: and forthwith they sprung up, because they had no deepness of earth: and when the sun was up, they were scorched; and because they had no root, they withered away. And some fell among thorns; and the thorns sprung up, and choked them: but other fell into good ground, and brought forth fruit, some an hundredfold, some sixtyfold, some thirtyfold. Who hath ears to hear, let him hear. . . .

Hear ye therefore the *parable of the sower.* When any one heareth the word of the kingdom, and understandeth it not, then cometh the wicked one, and catcheth away that which was sown in his heart. This is he which received seed by the way side. But he that received the seed into stony places, the same is he that heareth the word, and anon with joy receiveth it; yet hath he not root in himself, but dureth for a while: for when tribulation or persecution ariseth because of the word, by and by he is offended. He also that received seed among the thorns is he that heareth the word; and the care of this world, and the deceitfulness of riches, choke the word, and he becometh unfruitful. But he that received seed into the good ground is he that heareth the word, and understandeth it; which also beareth fruit, and bringeth forth, some an hundredfold, some sixty, some thirty.

Another parable put he forth unto them, saying, The kingdom of heaven is likened unto a man which sowed good seed in his field: but while men slept, his enemy came and sowed tares among the wheat, and went his way. But when the blade was sprung up, and brought forth fruit, then appeared the tares also. So the servants of the householder came and said unto him, Sir, didst not thou sow good seed in thy field? from whence then hath it tares? He said unto them, An enemy hath done this. The servants said unto him, Wilt thou then that we go and gather them up? But he said, Nay; lest while ye gather up the tares, ye root up also the wheat with them. Let both grow together until the harvest: and in the time of harvest I will say to the reapers, Gather ye together first the tares, and bind them in bundles to burn them: but gather the wheat into my barn. . . .

All these things spake Jesus unto the multitude in parables; and without a parable spake he not unto them: that it might be fulfilled which was spoken by the prophet, saying, I will open my mouth in parables; I will utter things which have been kept secret from the foundation of the world. (Matthew 13:3–9; 18–30, 34–35; emphasis added.)

In our teaching, perhaps we can seek to instruct the way Jesus did through his parables. We can say, "A certain man by the name of Smith . . ." and then tell the story, whether it be a story of lack of fidelity, a story of faith, or some other principle. Then we can end the story either by making a clear declaration of the principle involved or by asking the question, "Which of these two men went to the Lord justified?"

JESUS TAUGHT USING TANGIBLE EXAMPLES

When Jesus taught he often used tangible examples that could readily be seen around him. For example, the disciples once came to Jesus and asked, "Who is the greatest in the kingdom of heaven?" Before answering their question, *"Jesus called a little child unto him, and set him in the midst of them."* Then he said,

Verily I say unto you, Except ye be converted, and become as little children, ye shall not enter into the kingdom of heaven. Whosoever therefore shall humble himself *as this little child,* the same is greatest in the kingdom of heaven. And whoso shall receive one such little child in my name receiveth me. But whoso shall offend one of these little ones which believe in me, it were better for him that *a millstone* were hanged about his neck, and that he were drowned in the *depth of the sea.* (Matthew 18:1–6; emphasis added.)

On another occasion, the Pharisees "took counsel how they might entangle him in his talk. And they sent out unto him their disciples with the Herodians, saying, Master, we know that thou art true, and teachest the way of God in truth, neither carest thou for any man: for thou regardest not the person of men. Tell us therefore, What thinkest thou? Is it lawful to give tribute unto Caesar, or not?" Jesus saw through their trickery, and said,

Why tempt ye me, ye hypocrites? *Shew me the tribute money. And they brought unto him a penny.* And he saith unto them, Whose is this image and superscription? They say unto him, Caesar's. Then saith he unto them, Render therefore unto Caesar the things which are Caesar's; and unto God the things that are God's. When they had heard these words, they marvelled, and left him, and went their way. (Matthew 22:15–22; emphasis added.)

The non-Mormon scholar Frederic William Farrar, often quoted by Elder Bruce R. McConkie in *The Mortal Messiah,* gave this insight into the teaching of Jesus:

"How exquisitely and freshly simple is the actual language of Christ compared with all other teaching that has ever gained the ear of the world! . . . All is short, clear, precise, full of holiness, full of the common images of daily life.

"There is scarcely a scene or object familiar to the Galilee of that day, which Jesus did not use as a moral illustration of some glorious promise or moral law. He spoke of green fields, and springing flowers, and the budding of the vernal trees; of the red or lowering sky; of sunrise and sunset; of wind and rain; of night and storm; of clouds and lightning; of stream and river; of stars and lamps; of honey and salt; of quivering bulrushes and burning weeds; of rent garments and bursting wine-skins; of eggs and serpents; of pearls and pieces of money; of nets and fish. Wine and wheat, corn and oil, stewards and gardeners, laborers and employers, kings and shepherds, travellers and fathers of families, courtiers in soft clothing and brides in nuptial robes—all these are found in His discourses. He knew all life, and had gazed on it with a kindly as well as a kingly glance. He could sympathize with its joys no less than He could heal its sorrows, and the eyes that were so often suffused with tears as they saw the sufferings of earth's mourners beside the bed of death, had shone also with a kindlier glow as they watched the games of earth's happy little ones in the green fields and busy streets" (Farrar, *Life of Christ,* 204–5; quoted in McConkie, *The Mortal Messiah,* 4 vols. [Salt Lake City: Deseret Book Co., 1979–81], 2:180–81).

Jesus Taught to the People's Level of Readiness

Jesus knew all things, but he shared only that which was appropriate to his listener's level of understanding. In other words, he shared with people that which would lead them a step higher, but in no case did he try to unload all that he knew. Sometimes he must have wished that the people might be prepared to receive more—but never did he cross the line in teaching that which they were not ready to receive.

A good example of this principle can be found in his use of parables. After Jesus taught the parable of the sower and the seeds (Matthew 13:3–9), his disciples asked, "Why speakest thou unto them in parables?"

> He answered and said unto them, Because it is given unto you to know the mysteries of the kingdom of heaven, but to them it is not given. For whosoever hath, to him shall be given, and he shall have more abundance: but whosoever hath not, from him shall be taken away even that he hath. Therefore speak I to them in parables: because they seeing see not; and hearing they hear not, neither do they understand. And in them is fulfilled the prophecy of Esaias, which saith, By hearing ye shall hear, and shall not understand; and seeing ye shall see, and shall not perceive: For this people's heart is waxed gross, and their ears are dull of hearing, and their eyes they have closed; lest at any time they should see with their eyes, and hear with their ears, and should understand with their heart, and should be converted, and I should heal them.

> But blessed are your eyes, for they see: and your ears, for they hear. For verily I say unto you, That many prophets and righteous men have desired to see those things which ye see, and have not seen them; and to hear those things which ye hear, and have not heard them. (Matthew 13:10–17.)

Then, because they were ready, Jesus interpreted for them the meaning of the parable of the sower.

JESUS TAUGHT BY THE SPIRIT

It is helpful to see the variety of approaches Jesus used in his teaching. In all that he did he acted to perfection, and we can learn much from his style of teaching. But underlying all his teaching was this truth: He always taught by the Spirit.

Near the beginning of the Savior's mortal ministry, he visited the synagogue in Nazareth and took a turn at preaching to the people. Reading from the book of Isaiah, he bore testimony of himself by saying, "The Spirit of the Lord is upon me, because he hath anointed me to preach the gospel" (see Luke 4:18; see also Isaiah 61:1). Elsewhere, the Lord spoke through Isaiah of the mortal Messiah to say, "I have put my spirit upon him" (Isaiah 42:1; see also Matthew 12:18).

Elder Bruce R. McConkie bore testimony of this truth when he said: "Being without sin—being clean and pure and spotless—he was entitled to the constant companionship of the Holy Spirit. . . . He enjoyed, at all times, the fulness of that light and guidance and power which comes by the power of the Holy Ghost to the faithful" (*Mortal Messiah*, 1:369–70).

"Never man spake as we have just heard the Lord Jesus speak [in Matthew 7:28–29]. . . . 'He taught them as one having authority from God, and not as having authority from the scribes.' His . . . words, spoken by the power of the Holy Ghost, were the words of his Father" (*Mortal Messiah*, 2:177).

If Jesus, the greatest of all, needed to teach by the Spirit, how much more do we in our weakness need that heavenly help?

Jesus said:

I do nothing of myself; but as my Father hath taught me, I speak these things. (John 8:28.)

For I have not spoken of myself; but the Father which sent me, he gave me a commandment, what I should say, and what I should speak. (John 12:49)

The words that I speak unto you I speak not of myself: but the Father that dwelleth in me, he doeth the works. (John 14:10.)

As we seek to teach in the model given us by the Savior, let us follow his example in teaching by the Spirit, never relying only upon our own wisdom or knowledge or ability, but always, to the best of our ability, also letting the Father teach us, speak through us, and do his mighty work through us.

TESTIMONIES OF TEACHING BY THE SPIRIT

As we conclude this discussion, I would like to share two testimonies of latter-day apostles, Elder Bruce R. McConkie and Elder Dallin H. Oaks.

Bruce R. McConkie:

"Every teacher in every teaching situation might well reason along this line:

"If the Lord Jesus were here, what he would say in this situation would be perfect.

"But he is not here. Instead he has sent me to represent him.

"I should say what he would say if he were here; I should say what he wants said.

"The only way I can do this is to have him tell me what to say.

"This revealed direction can come to me only by the power of his Spirit.

"Therefore I must be guided by the Spirit if I am to teach in my capacity as an agent of the Lord. . . .

"Let us make this clear. Even though what we teach is true, it is not of God unless it is taught by the power of the Spirit. There is no conversion, no spiritual experience, unless the Spirit of the Lord is involved" ("The Teacher's Divine Commission," *Ensign,* Apr. 1979, 23–24; emphasis added).

"If you teach the word of truth—now note, you're saying what is true, every thing you say is accurate and right—by some other way than the Spirit, it is not of God. Now what is the other way to teach than by the Spirit? Well, obviously, it is by the power of the intellect.

"Suppose I came here tonight and delivered a great message on teaching, and I did it by the power of the intellect without any of the Spirit of God attending. Suppose that every word that I said was true, no error whatever, but it was an intellectual presentation. This revelation says: 'If it be by some other way it is not of God' (D&C 50:18).

"That is, God did not present the message through me because I used the power of the intellect instead of the power of the Spirit. Intellectual things—reason and logic—can do some good, and they can prepare the way, and they can get the mind ready to receive the Spirit under certain circumstances. But conversion comes and the truth sinks into the hearts of people only when it is taught by the power of the Spirit" (*The Foolishness of Teaching,* pamphlet [Salt Lake City: The Church of Jesus Christ of Latter-day Saints, 1981], 9).

Dallin H. Oaks:

"If we teach in the manner the Lord has prescribed, he can send his Spirit to edify and enlighten those whom we teach. If we do not teach in his way—if we teach according to our own knowledge and according to our own intellect, and if we slavishly tie ourselves to our own preparation or to someone else's wisdom or text—our teaching 'is not of God.' . . .

"If we rely on debate techniques or sales methods or group psychology, we are preaching the gospel in some other way, and it is not of God. . . .

"Intellectual things—reason and logic—can prepare the way, and they can help us in our preparation. But if we are tied to them instead of to the Spirit of the Lord, we are not teaching the gospel in the Lord's way.

"The Lord stressed that truth when he said: 'Put your trust in that Spirit which leadeth to do good—yea, to do justly, to walk humbly, to judge righteously; and this is my Spirit' (D&C 11:12).

"This is the way we must teach the gospel" ("Teaching and Learning by the Spirit," *Ensign,* Mar. 1997, 8–9).

QUESTIONS TO PONDER

1. What are some of the ways that we might at times teach the truth but not do so by the Spirit, and thus our teaching is not of the Lord?

---

2. Why is it so important to recognize that the *primary role* of a teacher is to try to prepare the spiritual environment around a "student" so he might have a spiritual experience with the Lord?

---

3. Why is it so difficult for most of us to believe the Lord will speak through us?

---

4. Why is it hard for some of us to believe and trust in the Lord as the Teacher? Why do we instead have the tendency to jump in and teach, train, and instruct others with our own understanding and our own wisdom?

---

5. When you are teaching, what could you do differently or better to help turn the listener to the Lord?

_____

_____

_____

6. How could you better apply some of the methods used by the Master Teacher in your teaching?

_____

_____

_____

CHAPTER 3

KEYS TO TEACHING
BY THE SPIRIT

When I was a young returned missionary, I was asked to travel around the stake (as most returned missionaries are) and speak in the wards about missionary work. After each talk the gracious members of the wards would come up to me and say, "Oh, that was such a good talk, Brother Cook. Thank you for coming." Unfortunately, after hearing such compliments a few times I began to believe them. Rather than give credit to the Lord, I began to take credit to myself.

One Sunday after I had received a number of compliments, an older man lingered behind the others and said to me, "Brother Cook, do you want to learn something?" I could tell from the tone of his voice that he meant business. I said, "Well, sure." But he seemed to doubt my answer. He repeated himself: "No. Do you *really* want to learn something?" I said again, "Well, yes, I would like to if you have something you'd like to share." He paused for a moment and then asked, "Brother Cook, why is it that you don't believe in teaching by the Spirit?"

I didn't know what to say. I struggled with how to respond to him, and then said awkwardly, "Well, I'm probably not as good at it as I should be, but I sure prayed over my talk and I tried to get prepared." He answered, "No, you don't know anything about it. Am I right to think you have an outline of your

talk on a notecard in your pocket?" I nodded. He said, "I'll tell
you what's on your notecard: At first you told them a joke, and
then related a story, then repeated a scripture. You had your
talk outlined in such perfect order that if the Lord had wanted
to say something through you he wouldn't have had a chance."

I was astonished. I didn't know what to say.

Then he said, "Please open your Doctrine and Covenants
to section 84, verse 85, and read it to me." This is what it says:

> Neither take ye thought beforehand what ye shall say;
> but treasure up in your minds continually the words of
> life, and it shall be given you in the very hour that portion
> that shall be meted unto every man.

"Well, I just thought you'd want to know what the Lord
says," he concluded, and he walked away. He left me with a
strange combination of feelings. For example, I was feeling a bit
of anger. Who is this guy anyway? What makes him such an
authority on speaking? Another feeling was defensiveness.
Surely the Lord wouldn't want me to stand up in a meeting
without any notes and give a talk without preparation, would
he? The General Authorities don't do that! They stand up in
conference and read their talks. (I wasn't thinking of the need
for an advance copy of conference talks for translation
purposes.)

I felt quite upset as I drove home, and the unsettled feelings
continued for days. I was still struggling later that week when
the bishop of my own ward called. "Gene, the main speaker in
our sacrament meeting this Sunday is sick. We want you to
speak for twenty-five minutes. Pick any subject you want." I
said, "Bishop, you know I gave my homecoming address in our
ward just a few weeks ago. The ward members just heard from
me." I did my very best to talk him out of the assignment,
mostly because of my continuing feelings of terrible unrest. But

he wouldn't change his mind, and I knew I was in trouble. I still remember the sick feeling that crept into my stomach.

As the days progressed, I continued to be troubled by doubts and fears. Unrighteous thoughts continued to plague me. Why should I be expected to speak without taking thought beforehand? Was I really expected to stand up in sacrament meeting for twenty-five minutes without a card or outline or anything? That seemed ridiculous—or foolish. Besides, I thought, your girlfriend is in this ward. And Dad will be there, and he'll be very disappointed in me if I "blow it." And if I try speaking without specific preparation or notes, I surely will blow it.

Unfortunately, that's where I was in my faith in those days, and you have to start progressing from where you are. I worried and prayed about what I was going to do. I thought that perhaps I would outline a talk and then leave the outline at home so that I would have a rough idea of what to say. I tried to select a topic, but I could not do it. I wrestled with one idea and then with another and I just could not feel good about any of them. The days kept clicking off until it got down to the day before, and I still couldn't settle on anything. I then descended to the lowest point in my faith during that experience when I finally said in my heart, "All right, I am going to get up there and try it, but just in case, I will have a spare talk in my pocket!" And then I heard the Spirit say, "Gene, do you believe or do you not? It is that simple." I had to say in my heart, "Yes, I believe."

So I didn't plan anything for my talk. I just read the scriptures. And I truly tried to humble myself to the dust. I prayed mightily that the Lord would help me and not just leave me standing there at the pulpit without anything to say. I prayed through that night. I fervently prayed the next morning.

It was all I could do to keep from thinking during the sacrament, "Now listen, you crazy guy, you have got to settle on something. At least think of a topic and a few ideas—a couple of stories or something. You have only five more minutes and you are on!" But I resisted the temptation, saying to myself, "No, if the Lord is capable of giving a talk through me, then he's capable of selecting a subject as well." I will never forget walking up to that podium, knowing that my mind was empty. I was really exercising my faith, and I prayed, "Heavenly Father, if you don't come through on this one I am done!" I really prayed with all of my heart.

As I began my talk, I'm sure I wandered around for two or three minutes: "Brothers and sisters, it's good to be in the ward. We have such a wonderful bishop. I'm so grateful for the gospel." I felt like I was marking time, not saying anything of substance—and I continued to pray with all my heart that the Lord would somehow impress upon me what I should speak about.

Then as I stood up there I felt something come over me that just carried me away, and I spoke by the Spirit of the Lord. To this day, I do not know what that talk was about, but it was a great spiritual witness to me that the Lord will work with us if we let him. I felt good about that talk because I felt that the Lord had given me what to say, and after the talk a number of people were moved to repent by the Spirit, who worked through me in that instance. Several people said, "Brother Cook, what happened to you? I felt something that has caused me literally to change. I will never be the same."

One man said to me, "Brother Cook, do you know that you quoted nearly a full paragraph right out of my patriarchal blessing?" And then he told me what was in the paragraph and how it had helped him understand his blessing.

A woman came up and said, "For years I have prayed and prayed to have an answer to a particular question. Right in the middle of your talk the Lord gave me the answer." And then she told me, through her tears, what the Lord had said to her.

A man came up and said, "Brother Cook, I have done some things in my life that were very wrong, and I have kept them carefully hidden from others. I have never been willing to go to a bishop and confess. I want you to know that while you were speaking, I heard the Lord tell me to go to the bishop. I am going to go."

It was a great witness to me that if we exercise our faith in the Lord, he will honor his words. I learned what the prophet Micaiah learned, that we need to have this attitude:

> As the Lord liveth, what the Lord saith unto me, that will I speak. (1 Kings 22:14.)

From that day to this, I have never written a talk out unless I've been required to. I really do believe that if you believe, the Lord will speak through you to the needs of the people. I bear testimony that he will work with us as he did with Enoch, when he said,

> Go forth and do as I have commanded thee, and no man shall pierce thee. Open thy mouth, and it shall be filled, and I will give thee utterance, for all flesh is in my hands, and I will do as seemeth me good. (Moses 6:32.)

This experience seems to typify for me some of the key elements of teaching by the Spirit. I believe that in its essence, teaching by the Spirit consists in large part of preparing your heart, humbling yourself, praying, and treasuring up the word, and then, when appropriate, preparing specific thoughts (but even when this is appropriate, such preparation should be secondary to these other principles). Finally, when you stand to speak or teach, pray continually that you will be able to do so with the Spirit.

With that introduction, let's look at some specific principles of speaking and teaching by the Spirit. (Some of the following ideas deal with preparing our hearts before the meeting. For other principles dealing with preparation, see chapter 4.)

BEFORE THE TALK OR LESSON

We Speak for the Lord

It is a weighty matter to understand that in Church settings the Lord expects us to speak for him, speaking by the power of the Spirit and in his name. We therefore need to truly see ourselves as instruments in the hands of God to touch the hearts of others. Each time I stand to speak or teach, I remind myself, "I am about to speak for Christ, and in his name." The enabling power of Christ then allows me to represent him with confidence.

In Jesus' teaching, he always recognized that he represented his Father. For example, he taught,

> My doctrine is not mine, but his that sent me. If any man will do his will, he shall know of the doctrine, whether it be of God, or whether I speak of myself. He that speaketh of himself seeketh his own glory: but he that seeketh his glory that sent him, the same is true, and no unrighteousness is in him. (John 7:16–18.)

Jesus teaches here that if a person speaks for himself, he seeks his own glory. But if a person truly seeks the glory of God, the one who sent him, then we can know that the messenger himself is true and there is no unrighteousness in him because his motives are pure. I like to think of a gospel teacher as somewhat like an ambassador. An ambassador is not to have any public views of his own; he represents only that which he is given by the leaders of his government.

The Lord gave a similar commission to his servants in the early days of the Church:

Therefore, verily I say unto you, lift up your voices unto this people; speak the thoughts that I shall put into your hearts, and you shall not be confounded before men; for it shall be given you in the very hour, yea, in the very moment, what ye shall say.

But a commandment I give unto you, that ye shall declare whatsoever thing ye declare in my name, in solemnity of heart, in the spirit of meekness, in all things. And I give unto you this promise, that inasmuch as ye do this the Holy Ghost shall be shed forth in bearing record unto all things whatsoever ye shall say. (D&C 100:5–8.)

These instructions apply to all who serve in the kingdom. We should not express our own opinions or feelings in our teaching. We are in the teaching setting to speak for the Lord, and to speak as directed by the leaders of the Church. Of course, we can use our own experiences to teach and to show how the teachings can be applied. But we must actively seek to learn what the Lord and the presiding Brethren desire, and that is what we ought to teach—nothing more, nothing less.

Every meeting in the Church is convened in the name of the Lord Jesus Christ. We pray in his name; we sing in his name. Any person who teaches, participates, or does anything in that meeting is to "speak in the name of God the Lord, even the Savior of the world; that faith also might increase in the earth; that mine everlasting covenant might be established" (D&C 1:20–22).

Speaking for and in the name of Christ is so important that the Lord has repeatedly counseled us to do so:

All things must be done in the name of Christ, whatsoever you do in the Spirit. (D&C 46:31.)

Whatsoever ye shall do, ye shall do it in my name. (3 Nephi 27:7.)

> Behold, the voice of the Lord came unto him, that he should return again, and prophesy unto the people whatsoever things should come into his heart. . . . And he said unto them: Behold, I, Samuel, a Lamanite, do speak the words of the Lord which he doth put into my heart. (Helaman 13:3, 5.)

Trust in the Lord

Another key is to trust in the Lord, believing that he will help you succeed in your teaching. In my experience of speaking without even knowing the subject in advance, at first I failed to trust—but when I repented and began to trust in the Lord, the blessing came. This kind of trust means you have to really believe that the Lord will work through you, however weak you may feel. The scriptures teach the vital importance of this kind of trust:

> Whatsoever thing ye shall ask in faith, believing that ye shall receive in the name of Christ, ye shall receive it. (Enos 1:15)

> If ye will not nourish the word, looking forward with an eye of faith to the fruit thereof, ye can never pluck of the fruit of the tree of life. (Alma 32:40.)

> Let us therefore come boldly unto the throne of grace, that we may obtain mercy, and find grace to help in time of need. (Hebrews 4:16.)

> Therefore, dearly beloved brethren, let us cheerfully do all things that lie in our power; and then may we stand still, with the utmost assurance, to see the salvation of God, and for his arm to be revealed. (D&C 123:17.)

Pray

Prayer is a critical element in this process. I was absolutely stuck until I humbled myself and began to pray. Then it seemed like I prayed nonstop during every waking moment until I stood to speak—and then I continued to pray in my heart, pleading for help with my assignment.

Again, the Lord gives us guidance and encouragement through the scriptures:

> Behold, I say unto you that ye must pray always, and not faint; that ye must not perform any thing unto the Lord save in the first place ye shall pray unto the Father in the name of Christ, that he will consecrate thy performance unto thee, that thy performance may be for the welfare of thy soul. (2 Nephi 32:9.)

> Behold, I say unto you that whoso believeth in Christ, doubting nothing, whatsoever he shall ask the Father in the name of Christ it shall be granted him; and this promise is unto all, even unto the ends of the earth. . . . O then despise not, and wonder not, but hearken unto the words of the Lord, and ask the Father in the name of Jesus for what things soever ye shall stand in need. Doubt not, but be believing. (Mormon 9:21, 27.)

> Whatsoever ye shall ask the Father in my name, which is right, believing that ye shall receive, behold it shall be given unto you. (3 Nephi 18:20.)

> Cry unto God for all thy support; yea, let all thy doings be unto the Lord, and whithersoever thou goest let it be in the Lord; yea, let all thy thoughts be directed unto the Lord; yea, let the affections of thy heart be placed upon the Lord forever. Counsel with the Lord in all thy doings, and he will direct thee for good. (Alma 37:36–37.)

Humble Yourself to the Dust

Elder Richard G. Scott of the Quorum of the Twelve taught of the difference between a humble person who allows the

Holy Ghost to teach and a proud person who relies on his or her own strength:

"Some years ago I had an assignment in Mexico and Central America similar to that of an Area President. . . .

"One Sunday, . . . I visited [a] branch priesthood meeting where a humble, unschooled Mexican priesthood leader struggled to communicate truths of the gospel. It was obvious how deeply they had touched his life. I noted his intense desire to communicate those principles. He recognized they were of great worth to the brethren he loved. He read from the lesson manual, yet his manner was of pure love of the Savior and those he taught. That love, sincerity, and purity of intent allowed the influence of the Holy Ghost to envelop the room. . . .

"Subsequently, I visited the Sunday School class in the ward where my family attended. A well-educated university professor presented the lesson. That experience was in striking contrast to the one enjoyed in the branch priesthood meeting. It seemed to me that the instructor had purposely chosen obscure references and unusual examples to develop his assigned topic—the life of Joseph Smith. I had the distinct impression that he used the teaching opportunity to impress the class with his great knowledge. . . . He did not seem as intent on communicating principles as had the humble priesthood leader. . . .

" . . . The humility of the Mexican priesthood leader was requisite to his being used as an instrument for spiritual communication of truth" (*Helping Others to Be Spiritually Led*, address to religious educators, 11 Aug. 1998, 10–12).

When I relied on my own abilities as a speaker, I was being somewhat prideful without realizing it. But when I humbled myself and acknowledged my true dependence on the Lord, I was able to become his instrument, and the Spirit spoke through me.

The Book of Mormon gives us another example of the need

for humility. When a Lamanite king desired spiritual blessings, Aaron counseled him, "If thou desirest this thing, if thou wilt *bow down* before God, yea, if thou wilt repent of all thy sins, and will *bow down* before God, and call on his name in faith, believing that ye shall receive, then shalt thou receive the hope which thou desirest" (Alma 22:16; emphasis added). The king then did as Aaron instructed: repenting, humbling himself, and praying in faith—and great blessings followed (see Alma 22:17–25; 23:1–7).

Treasure Up the Word

"Neither take ye thought beforehand what ye shall say," the Lord counsels, "but treasure up in your minds continually the words of life, and it shall be given you in the very hour that portion that shall be meted unto every man" (D&C 84:85).

And again:

> Seek not to declare my word, but first seek to obtain my word, and then shall your tongue be loosed; then, if you desire, you shall have my Spirit and my word, yea, the power of God unto the convincing of men. (D&C 11:21.)

This gives us two of the most important things we can do to help us teach by the Spirit: first, we need to not get too tied to a particular concept or outline (unless the Lord has given us direction in advance); second, we need to "continually" be studying the scriptures, and seeking to learn and understand the Lord's word. As we "treasure up . . . the words of life," we will be building a storehouse from which we can draw, with the help of the Spirit, when the time comes to teach or speak.

Do All in Your Power; Then Rely on the Grace of the Lord

When we seek to follow the Lord's pattern for teaching by the Spirit, we can then have confidence that he will help us in our efforts. We should have great hope in knowing, however unworthy we may feel or weak we may be, that if we will do all we can, he will come to our aid and provide for us whatever we may lack (see 2 Corinthians 12:9). That statement, to some degree, defines grace.

One of the definitions of grace is a "divine means of help or strength, given through the bounteous mercy and love of Jesus Christ." It is "an enabling power." (Bible Dictionary, 697.) The doctrine of the grace of the Father and the Son and how it affects us is so significant that it is mentioned more than two hundred times in the standard works.

This grace, or enabling power, is accessed by faith (see Romans 5:1–2). No wonder faith in the Lord Jesus Christ is the first principle of the gospel.

How clear was Christ's question to a sinking Peter, after he had walked on the water: "'O thou of little faith, wherefore didst thou doubt?" (Matthew 14:31). The moment Peter doubted and took his eyes off the Savior, he severed himself from the power of Jesus Christ that had sustained him on the water.

How many times, likewise, as we have prayed for assistance or help with our assignments, have we severed ourselves from the power of God because of doubt or fear, and thus could not obtain this enabling power of God? (See D&C 6:36; 67:3.)

Doing all in your own power is a necessary prerequisite to receiving grace. Truly did Paul teach, "By grace are ye saved through faith; and that not of yourselves: it is the gift of God: Not of works, lest any man should boast" (Ephesians 2:8–9). Yes, works alone cannot bring that divine gift, but they are a key condition upon which the gift is received (see 2 Nephi 10:23–25). "For we know that it is by grace that we are saved, after all we can do" (2 Nephi 25:23).

Unless one has done all in his own power, he cannot expect the grace of God to be manifest. What a glorious principle to understand: the Lord's assistance to us—whether we have strong faith or weak faith; whether a man, a woman, or a child—is not based just on what we know, how strong we are, or who we are, but more upon our giving all that we can give and doing all that we can do in our present circumstances. Once one has given all he can, then the Lord, through His grace, may assist him (see D&C 123:17). Clearly, the Lord's role and our role in our receiving divine help come into clear perspective in these inspired words: "I can do all things through Christ which strengtheneth me" (Philippians 4:13).

So it is with us as teachers. When we do all that we can, we will "receive the grace of God, that [we] might wax strong in the Spirit, . . . that [we] might teach with power and authority from God" (Mosiah 18:26).

TEACHING OR SPEAKING WITH THE SPIRIT

Speak "in the Moment"

"Lift up your voices unto this people," the Lord has said; "speak the thoughts that I shall put into your hearts, and you shall not be confounded before men; for it shall be given you in the very hour, yea, in the very moment, what ye shall say" (D&C 100:5–6).

This may be the ultimate in teaching by the Spirit: to totally put ourselves in the hands of the Lord and to let him guide us, even if that guidance doesn't come until the last minute.

How will we know what to say when we're teaching or speaking? The Lord will tell us through his Spirit. He will help us to feel and understand what he would have us say; and when we're following that Spirit, we "shall not be confounded before men."

This is the lesson the elderly brother was trying to teach me when I was a young returned missionary. If you plan your talk or your lesson out too tightly, even though your preparation may be excellent, you may not be allowing the Lord the opportunity to speak through you, giving you guidance "in the very moment" you stand before the class or congregation. This does not mean that you can't plan things out, that you can't think through what you might do with your lesson, that you can't write down a few ideas. But it does mean that you should be open to the impressions and feelings the Lord would send to you at the last minute.

Over the years I've watched a number of the Brethren as they sit on the stand waiting to be called on to speak. Many times they won't have a clue of what they're going to talk about, even when it's almost time for them to stand and speak. I've had that same experience myself. Sometimes my turn to speak is just moments away, and I will find that my mind is absolutely blank. That's when you start praying more fervently! Then perhaps a single word will come, or a feeling, or an impression about an individual in the audience. I will quickly make a note or two and then stand up and the Lord will help me to know what to say.

Again, it may be appropriate to plan in advance what you might say. If you're teaching a class during the Sunday block of your Church meetings, for example, you've been instructed to follow the manual and teach from the scriptures. So you make an outline, seeking the Lord's inspiration on how to teach the material you've been assigned. Sometimes you'll go to the class on Sunday and present the lesson precisely as you have planned it. But my experience is that often, in the very moment when you're teaching, something will happen in the class that will cause you to go in a different direction from what you had planned. You must follow those impressions.

When the Spirit leads you away from your notes or outline, don't worry about forgetting something important you wanted to say. If it truly is of the Lord, he will cause the idea to come back to you.

I like what Elder Bruce R. McConkie once said to me about being guided "in the moment." "What I've learned," he said, "is that you just stand up and start talking and pray and wait." Then he added, "Sometimes I'll kind of wander around for a little while. Then all of the sudden there's this feeling—*that's it!* And then you go right after some theme that you've been impressed with. I've seen the impressions come from a variety of sources. But you have to believe the Lord will help you, and you have to be seeking, searching, watching, and waiting. And then the Lord helps."

To speak better in the moment, we must listen before we speak. We must seek before we speak. If we do, we'll be able to speak by the Spirit.

One local leader shared with me this experience of a father who followed the Spirit in speaking "in the moment":

"Recently a tough teenage football player and his father helped a neighbor move a piano. This young man impressed everyone with his physical strength. He handled one end of the piano alone, while it took three grown men to manage the other end. Everyone complimented him and admired him for what it took to get his body into that kind of shape.

"Afterward, on the way home in the car, the father recognized a good teaching moment and bore testimony to his son that just as physical prowess comes from constant exercise and conditioning, so does one's spiritual prowess. He challenged his son to ask the Lord how he might be able to do that. The son responded with a typical teenager's 'Yeah, yeah, Dad, I've heard it all before' attitude, and the father assumed his comments had fallen on deaf ears.

"The next day, however, in fast and testimony meeting, this son related that after hearing his father's comment he began to ponder it and decided to pray about it. He then tearfully bore witness to the ward that the Spirit whispered to him a plan of action to get his spiritual life in order. He is now preparing for a mission. Thank goodness for a father who knew how to teach by the Spirit!"

Teach the Doctrine

We are to go out and teach the doctrine of the kingdom. It is truth, not falsehood, that changes lives. In the example of the tough, football-playing son, the father not only spoke by the Spirit "in the moment," but he also bore testimony of truth.

We read in Jacob 7:24 that "many means were devised to reclaim and restore the Lamanites to the knowledge of the truth; but it all was vain." Sometimes we in the Church try to devise many means to "reclaim and restore" the less-active members, or to reach those who come to Sunday classes and sacrament meetings. We develop programs and approaches— but too often, it seems, "it all [is] vain."

In Alma, however, we find an approach that bore fruit.

> [Alma] did . . . go forth among his people, or among the people of Nephi, that he might preach the word of God unto them, to stir them up in remembrance of their duty, and that he might pull down, *by the word of God,* all the pride and craftiness and all the contentions which were among his people, seeing no way that he might reclaim them save it were in *bearing down in pure testimony* against them" (Alma 4:19; emphasis added).

Some years later, Alma used the same approach:

> And now, as the *preaching of the word had a great tendency to lead the people to do that which was just*—yea, it had had more powerful effect upon the minds of the people than the sword, or anything else, which had happened unto them—therefore Alma thought it was

expedient that they should *try the virtue of the word of God.* (Alma 31:5; emphasis added.)

So have we been commanded in our day:

> At all times, and in all places, he [Oliver Cowdery—but this is true of all of us] shall open his mouth and declare my gospel as with the voice of a trump, both day and night. And I will give unto him strength such as is not known among men. (D&C 24:12.)

I bear witness that the Lord has given these passages by revelation. If we will preach the doctrine that relates to the topics at hand, if we will preach from the scriptures, the truth will be distilled as the dews from heaven. And the promise is that if we will teach the doctrine, the Spirit of the Lord will attend us.

In our teaching of truth, we often consider children (and students of all ages) as *vessels to be filled*—when they really are *fires to be ignited.* In our premortal lives, the Lord taught us all things that were necessary in preparation for this life (see D&C 138:55–56). Therefore, in one sense, the challenge isn't so much to *teach* a person something as to help him *remember* what he once knew. It is only through the Spirit that this process can fully occur. Alexander Pope wrote:

> Men must be taught as if you taught them not
> And things unknown proposed as things forgot.

The Spirit will help us to know what truth to teach, and the Spirit will help the listener to receive the truth in his or her heart.

The Spirit will also help us to know what falsehoods to combat in our teaching. As teachers in the Church and in our homes, we are not only planting seeds, but we are also eliminating weeds.

In all of our teaching of truth, then, we need to be careful about what truth we teach. When Jesus said we should not cast holy things to the dogs or our pearls before swine (see Matthew 7:6), what he was really teaching was that sacred things ought not be given to those who are unworthy or unprepared. An inspired teacher will know what truths he can and cannot teach. As latter-day scripture says,

> For it is not meet that the things which belong to the children of the kingdom should be given to them that are not worthy or to dogs, or the pearls to be cast before swine. (D&C 41:6.)

SOME LIMITATIONS ON TEACHING THE TRUTH

In teaching the truth, we need to keep these principles in mind:

1. Some things are taught only to those who are worthy. Thus, even though they are true, they cannot be shared with all. The Savior taught parables to the unbelievers, more doctrine to the believers.

2. Some things, even though they are true, may be taught prematurely or at the wrong time and cause real sorrow or heartbreak. The proper timing of teaching may relate to age or understanding or the ability of the person receiving the truth to absorb it. Thus, truth must be said at the right moment and in the right way.

3. One level of learning must precede and build upon another. We must give people milk before they are ready for meat (see D&C 19:22).

> For behold, thus saith the Lord God: I will give unto the children of men line upon line, precept upon precept, here a little and there a little; and blessed are those who hearken unto my precepts, and lend an ear unto my counsel, for they shall learn wisdom; for unto him that

receiveth I will give more; and from them that shall say,
We have enough, from them shall be taken away even that
which they have. (2 Nephi 28:30.)

4. Even if something is truthful, it may not be right to speak
that truth. For example, the Lord knows when each person is
going to die, but in his wisdom he withholds that information
from most of us. Likewise, we may be required to withhold
information even though it is true.

5. Some things, even though they are true, have been
removed by repentance in the lives of people and are not to be
shared (for example, a father should not confess an earlier
immorality to his ten-year-old son).

6. There are some truths that the Lord commands not be
shared with men, specifically those having to do with evils
of the world that could be passed on from generation to
generation.

Teach in a Spirit of Love

Another key to teaching by the Spirit is to learn to focus on
the Lord and the class or congregation, and to forget ourselves.
That involves casting out fear and letting ourselves be filled
with love.

"Wo be unto them that shall pervert the ways of the Lord,"
Mormon said, " . . . for they shall perish except they repent.
Behold, I speak with boldness, having authority from God; and
I fear not what man can do; for perfect love casteth out all fear"
(Moroni 8:16). Because of his authority and his love, Mormon
was able to speak hard things to others, fearlessly.

In the Lord's list of attributes of a good servant, he men-
tions love twice (once as charity):

And faith, hope, charity and love, with an eye single
to the glory of God, qualify him for the work. (D&C 4:5.)

It has been said that people don't care how much you know until they know how much you care. If you want to learn how to share the scriptures better, you've first got to feel love for your students, and then they will be taught by you. Without love, understanding cannot flow effectively between two people. Love truly is the power that brings the Spirit into a teaching situation.

FOCUS ON THE NEEDS OF THE PEOPLE

I once attended a Gospel Doctrine class where the teacher was discussing the writings of Paul. He was very knowledgeable, knowing far more than most about his subject. But he seemed to care more about the information than he did about the needs of the people. Covering the material became the primary thing to accomplish in the lesson; meeting the people's needs didn't seem to be a consideration at all.

If we will focus on the needs of the people, trying to understand what the Lord would have us say to help them with those needs, the Spirit will come and help us in our teaching. To meet the people's needs we need to try to know them. That's not so hard when we're teaching in our own home or our own ward. But sometimes you'll be teaching in a setting where you don't know a soul. What can you do then? I offer two suggestions:

First, when you enter the room you can shake hands with some of the people, look in their eyes, and try to discern with the Spirit where they are spiritually and emotionally. Prayerfully ask as you meet the people, "Heavenly Father, is there anything I should know?" Sometimes as I've taken hold of someone's hand I've had an impression, "Be sure to touch on this issue or problem when you speak." In those experiences, the Lord has spoken something to me about the needs of the people, and once you understand the needs, you can better minister to the people. Some of my greatest teaching experiences have happened when I have come to sense a challenge or a problem in an audience that I wasn't aware of before I arrived. Then, because I recognized that need, the Lord spoke through me to bless the people.

Second, think about the particular needs of the people in your life, and see if those needs might be found in the class or congregation you'll be teaching. Sometimes deep needs can be found almost universally, and you can greatly bless others by addressing those needs through the Spirit.

When we consider ourselves as the teachers, we will likely fail to teach the specific things each student needs. But when we prayerfully teach with the Spirit, we will say the right thing at the right time, and the Spirit will convey the truth to each student who is spiritually ready. This is truly a remarkable process. When we teach of ourselves, we may communicate one lesson to the entire class. But when we speak or teach as directed by the Spirit, we may communicate as many lessons as there are students in the room.

One caution: Never be so worried about the needs of the people that it could overpower any needs the Lord might convey directly to you. As important as it is to determine the needs of the people, it is more important to determine what the Lord would have us do when we are teaching.

An example of this was related to me by the father of a missionary (I've changed the missionary's name and mission to protect his privacy):

"Several days after our son, John, left for the England London Mission, we received a call from his mission president indicating that John appeared to be suffering from depression. I was quite surprised. Even though John suffered from hyperactivity in the past, any depression he had was minor and short-lived.

"Over the next two days, we did all we could think of to support our son and help him to make the right choice. Then his president called again and indicated that John had expressed a real desire to return home. I came to believe that John was suffering more from fear of his own inadequacy and the change in culture rather than a clinical depression and that he would be all right if he could just get past the next several weeks. I had felt the same way the first several weeks of my mission, as had all of our other children who have served missions.

"John's mission president had given him permission to call us that day to discuss the matter with him. I am a born worrier and suffer from anxiety on occasions, so this experience was difficult for me. I prayed many times during that day to know what to say when John called. . . .

"Later that day we spoke to our son. Before he called I had made a list of several things I wanted to say to him. However, when I answered the phone, instead of lecturing him, I asked what he wanted from the conversation. He simply said, 'I just want some support.' I found that I was able to talk for about fifteen minutes, not even thinking about what I should say. I covered only one of the points I had written down, but found that the others were not needed. My son responded very positively, and at the end we had resolved that he would stick it out for at least another month. The Lord blessed me to sense what would work and what would not in our conversation. As I had felt earlier, I sensed that he was simply 'homesick' and needed time to adjust. He had never been away from home before—in fact, had never been outside of Utah—until he left for England.

"I believe that he will now stay and serve an honorable mission. But, even if he should choose to leave early, I believe that my prayers were answered and I was able to respond with what he needed. I am so thankful to the Lord for his help."

TEACH WITH FEELING

President Harold B. Lee used to say, "It's more important what you feel than what you know. You know you're beginning to be converted when your heart tells you things your mind doesn't know." The Lord normally speaks to us in our hearts and in our minds, through feelings and thoughts. However, of the two, I believe feelings are deeper and more imbued with the Spirit. And it is feelings more than thoughts that people remember from a teaching setting. An effective teacher will make certain that what is being taught invites the listener to experience appropriate feelings.

Feelings are what move people to action—to repent, to seek the Lord, to overcome a habit. We persuade people by reason, but we really motivate them through emotion, through their feelings. It is feelings, then, that help bring people to change and repentance. When preaching the gospel with the Spirit, it is not enough just to speak of repentance academically. Even when people know they ought to repent, they usually won't do so until they begin to *feel* repentant. It's the *feelings* from the Spirit that will make the difference—and the teacher can help promote feeling in a class or congregation by feeling deeply about the subject himself.

I had a personal experience with President Harold B. Lee that underscored these truths. In 1972 I attended the priesthood session of general conference in the Tabernacle. It was a great priesthood meeting, a unique experience. In that particular meeting President Lee taught very effectively and with great power that we ought to be obedient to the laws of the land, that we ought to pay our income tax. He talked specifically about adultery and gave some other instructions, stating things so clearly that nobody could misunderstand. It was a powerful meeting. As I sat in the audience listening by the Spirit, I had a

tremendous surge of feelings and a witness that a prophet of
the Lord was speaking.

I pondered on these things that night as I went home. The
next morning before the Tabernacle Choir broadcast, I parked
my car and started toward the walkway through the tunnel
under the Tabernacle. Because I was really thinking about what
had been said the night before, I was walking with my eyes
toward the ground—and almost bumped into President Lee on
the walkway. He was walking alone, which was unusual. He
said, "Come and join me and let's walk over together."

As we started walking I tried to express to him some of the
feelings I had had the night before. I had a hard time expressing
myself. I was rather emotional and couldn't quite get the words
out.

Finally he stopped me and said, "Gene, you don't need to
say any more. I know what you're trying to say and I understand it." Then he said, "May I share something with you?" He
said something that showed me the caliber of that prophet.
"There were a lot of things said last night that perhaps have not
been stated as clear policy before. I worked over those things
to be sure they were correct and right and that the presidency
was in agreement. But I wasn't worried much about those
things, other than that they be said correctly. What I was worried about was that I wanted every last priesthood holder to *feel*
in his heart the great witness and outpouring of the Spirit.
That's what I wanted, and it didn't matter as much what was
being taught, as long as they felt with great power the Spirit of
the Lord." He said then—and this is a great quote from him—
"Remember, Gene, it's more important what you *feel* than what
you know."

We walked on to the Tabernacle, and I sat down in the
audience. There was half an hour or so before the general
session was to begin. Because I was really impressed by what
President Lee had told me, I felt I ought to write it down. It

took about half an hour, and I wrote about four to six pages. When I was finished, the thought came to me, 'He couldn't have said all that—he was with me only three or four minutes."

Then I learned another great lesson. All those pages were from President Lee. He spoke to me in those few minutes in the Spirit in such a way that it was as if he had played an orchestra in perfect harmony inside of me spiritually. He played a hundred notes, though he used maybe only four. That's speaking by the Spirit. I learned some great things that day about how he did it with me and how you, by the Spirit, can play that harmony inside of others, moving them to repent, to put their lives in order.

Feelings are conveyed to the depths of our souls. We then remember them better and can teach from them.

When I was newly called as a General Authority, my seven-year-old son stood to bear his testimony in sacrament meeting. He had forgotten what a General Authority is; he couldn't even remember the words. All he could say was "My dad has been called to be a . . . , to be a . . . , to be one of those men who knows about Jesus." He couldn't remember the term, but he knew the *feeling*.

When you are teaching, do your best to teach in simple terms from your heart. Try hard not to be too intellectual or to be too academic about the way you are teaching, or it will decrease the people's ability to feel the things you are teaching about.

I believe that there are great truths in this statement: "If you are not feeling it as a teacher, they are probably not feeling it as the students."

Have you ever noticed in classrooms when someone begins to relate a personal example, illustration, or something that they feel deeply about, an "electricity" seems to permeate the entire room? People tend to sense and *feel* the message that is being conveyed. I have noticed through the years that if in the very process of teaching I am trying to humble myself, to be prayerful, and to focus on the needs of the people, that that very effort causes me to feel deeply what I am saying.

When one has a great love for others, he tends to be on the feeling level. Thus when he speaks, if he is filled with the love of God, he will speak on the feeling level, and people will feel in their hearts the words he is speaking.

It is important that people *feel* and not just understand in their minds that which you are teaching. Almost anyone can convey information to the mind. In order to convey to the heart through feeling, the one teaching must make a special effort to humble himself and become involved personally in the message. He must feel the spirit of what he is saying. When he does, that feeling quickly transmits to others.

Teaching to the mind is important—then understanding comes to people. But that is not enough. Added to understandings are feelings that touch people in their hearts. That will then lead to the third level of teaching: The combination of understanding and feeling will cause the learner to act. He will feel a need to change, will make a resolution, and then will begin to repent or move in the direction he knows the Lord would have him go.

I say once again that if you are not feeling it as a teacher, they are probably not feeling it as students. Your own feelings, then, can often be a good measure of how things may be going in a given teaching setting.

THE SPIRIT AND EMOTION

We have talked about the importance of feelings. However, I would like to add a caution here, because sometimes we feel that tears or overflowing emotions are signs of the Spirit's presence. That is not necessarily so. I'm grateful for these words of President Howard W. Hunter, who explained how we can discern different manifestations of the Spirit:

"I get concerned when it appears that strong emotion or free-flowing tears are equated with the presence of the Spirit. Certainly the Spirit of the Lord can bring strong emotional feelings, including tears, but that outward manifestation ought not to be confused with the presence of the Spirit itself.

"I have watched a great many of my brethren over the years and we have shared some rare and unspeakable spiritual experiences together. Those experiences have all been different, each special in its own way, and such sacred moments may or may not be accompanied by tears. Very often they are, but sometimes they are accompanied by total silence. Other times they are accompanied by joy. Always they are accompanied by a great manifestation of the truth, of revelation of the heart. . . .

"Listen for the truth, hearken to the doctrine, and let the manifestations of the Spirit come as it may in all of its many and varied forms. Stay with solid principles; teach from a pure heart. Then the Spirit will penetrate your mind and heart and every mind and heart of your students" ("Eternal Investments," address to religious educators, 10 Feb. 1989).

DRAW ON PERSONAL EXPERIENCE

As we discussed earlier, treasuring up the words of life involves regularly and deeply delving into the scriptures. But there is another thing we ought to be treasuring up: the experiences of our lives that can be helpful in teaching. When I receive a speaking or teaching assignment, I begin to pray for help that I can be more observant each day—I seek to notice better what's happening around me at home, at work, and elsewhere, looking for stories, illustrations, and examples I can use in the teaching assignment.

Because I become more prayerfully focused, I begin to see

more. The Lord begins to fill the reservoir upon which the Spirit can then draw in the teaching setting. Almost every day I'm able to see two or three things that might be valuable to use as stories or illustrations in teaching.

This is true of all of us. Whether we know it or not, we've had a myriad of experiences that can be helpful to draw on in our teaching. If we will ask and if we will focus our minds, the Lord can touch us and bring to mind an experience that we may not have thought of for many years. And perhaps there is someone in the class or congregation who will be greatly blessed by that experience.

One reason why personal experiences are so effective is that they have touched our hearts—and when we speak of things that we feel deeply, it is more likely that we'll be able to touch the hearts of others.

If you read a lesson and tell a story in someone else's words, it won't have the same impact.

In telling stories, be sure to shorten them to their essential elements. If you are telling an experience from your mission, you don't need to say who your companion was, where the experience took place, or any other such details. And be careful in telling personal stories not to bring too much focus to yourself or to relate experiences that are too personal.

APPLY THE TRUTHS

I believe that when the Holy Ghost teaches us something, it's normally not just for our information. The Spirit doesn't seem to spend a lot of time on purely academic issues. Instead, the Lord generally tells us things to help us to repent and do better in our lives.

We need to take the same approach in our teaching. One element of teaching by the Spirit is to apply the truths to the individuals in the class.

For example, after King Benjamin reminded his people of how he had served them, he added this application:

> I tell you these things that ye may learn wisdom; that ye may learn that when ye are in the service of your fellow beings ye are only in the service of your God. (Mosiah 2:17.)

Another example: Jesus taught his disciples that those who help others are helping him. And then he applied the lesson directly to his listeners (and readers):

> Verily I say unto you, Inasmuch as ye have done it unto one of the least of these my brethren, ye have done it unto me. (Matthew 25:40.)

So should we do in our teaching. It is not enough just to teach facts or to share information. We also need to liken the lessons to the lives of those we teach, so that they can apply the material to their own lives, so they can repent and be blessed.

EVEN A CHILD CAN DO IT

These principles of teaching by the Spirit are simple enough that even a child can apply them. When I was a new father I wondered how much a child could teach by the Spirit. I believed that if these principles were true, the Lord could help a child as readily as he could one of us—or perhaps even more easily, because children are more pure and innocent than adults are.

As each of our eight children has come along we've tried to teach them these principles from an early age. When they received a speaking assignment in Primary, we would have them talk through with us what they might do. We might help them to think of a story and example illustrating their talk. We might help them to find a scripture. And we would ask questions: How do you feel about this subject, son? Have you prayed about it? Have you prayed about the kids in Primary, to discover what they need? Do you have a testimony of what you're going to talk about? I've learned that little children can answer all those questions.

Years ago, when one of our sons was about eight years old (I'll call him John), he decided to tell the story of David and Goliath. He stood up there without notes and quoted a scripture he had memorized; he told of David and Goliath, and how David showed his willingness to trust in the Lord; and he related a little story of how the Lord had answered his own prayer. We talked him through the story so that he would be comfortable and feel prepared. Several times in the process I said, "Now, John, don't get stuck on what you've prepared. The Lord may give you feelings that you should do something different. He may add some things to your talk, or he may want you to take something out." John gave a talk without any notes, and tried to follow the Spirit as he did.

About an hour after my son had given his talk, one of the Primary teachers in the ward called my wife on the telephone. "Your son's talk was such an inspiration to me that we gathered our whole family together after church and we all decided we're going to begin reading the scriptures together as a family." She bore her testimony that in the middle of John's talk, the Spirit bore witness to her that that's what she should do. Now, more than a decade later, that woman and her family continue to be blessed through reading the scriptures as a family.

Why? Because a little child decided to try to teach by the Spirit. And if little John could do it, so can we all.

I first began to learn what it meant to teach by the Spirit when I was a young returned missionary giving talks in my home stake. In the years since, I have discovered the true power of this kind of partnership with God in our teaching. Visual aids, object lessons, stories, and other such helps all have their place in teaching, and all should be used as appropriate.

But it is only when we successfully invite the Spirit into our teaching that hearts and lives are changed; it is only through the Spirit that we are able to help our brothers and sisters grow closer to our Father in heaven.

SOME EXAMPLES FROM OTHERS

I would like to share some success stories that show these concepts at work in real life.

For instance, here is a wonderful letter I received from a stake president who was trying to apply these truths:

"We have tried to teach more fully by the Spirit in our training for the past year and a half, with some wonderful results. We still have a long way to go, but we are pleased with the progress so far. Following are some of our experiences.

"First, we committed ourselves as a stake presidency never again to have a prepared talk written out, but to 'prepare the messenger, not the message,' and speak from the heart as directed by the Spirit. We're trying hard to set the right example, and have had wonderful experiences of being told in the very moment what to say, feeling the Spirit stronger, and learning of lives being changed.

"For example, a young mother recently tearfully thanked me for a talk I gave about a year ago that has changed her life. I was prompted to speak more directly than I normally would about mothers staying home to be with their children. At that moment the Spirit told her it was time to make that change. She gave up a very promising career to follow the prompting. Now her marriage is stronger, her children are happier, she has discovered the incomparable joy of motherhood, and her life has never felt more fulfilled. She is now the ward Young Women president and is teaching those dear young women how to establish their priorities. The blessings that will flow as a result of her feeling that prompting could span generations.

"Second, we have spent hours teaching these principles to our high council. We have committed them to spend the extra effort required to prepare themselves to speak by the Spirit. (It really does require more preparation!) We encourage them to share their experiences in high council meeting to strengthen the less committed among them. One brother recently told us he now feels the Spirit having a more profound influence in his whole life, and that he rarely, if ever, attends any meeting where the Spirit does not whisper something to him.

"Some who used to struggle to deliver a talk are now among our most popular speakers. My own teenage daughter recently shared over Sunday dinner an experience she had during sacrament meeting where she received an answer from the Spirit to a problem that had been vexing her. I was pleasantly surprised to learn that the speaker was one of the last of our high councilors to make the commitment to leave his written talks at home. He delivered this talk without a single note! My daughter said it was the best sacrament meeting talk she had ever heard.

"Third, our bishoprics have accepted the challenge to always seek to speak by the Spirit, and to take the extra time to teach and challenge every sacrament meeting speaker to do the same. . . . We believe that sacrament meetings should be times of personal revelation, and this means the Spirit must be there in abundance.

"We have a long way to go in this area, but are making good progress. We believe that 'if you build it, they will come,' that if the people are fed in sacrament meeting, their lives will be changed, their performance in their Church callings will improve, and the Lord will prompt the less-active members and nonmembers to come to be fed.

"Someone recently told me she was seeing less-active members 'fall from the trees' and suddenly appear in church on Sunday, often without any invitation from other members.

We've sent five or six couples to the temple in the past year from this ward. All it took was spiritual sacrament meetings, loving people, and a good elders quorum president who knows how to teach by the Spirit.

"Fourth, we are trying to teach our people to come prepared to be fed by the Spirit, and to 'pray their way through the meeting.' We've done this in stake conference talks, ward conferences, and leadership meetings. We're trying to get people to arrive early (a really big challenge in our stake!), and to be more reverent, especially in sacrament meeting. I can't claim a lot of success here yet, but it will come as we continue to lovingly teach and set the right example.

"One brother recently told me after a leadership meeting, 'That was the best leadership meeting I've ever attended!' I responded, 'Do you know who's responsible for that? You are! You came prepared to feel the Spirit.' His eyes teared up and he said, 'Yes, I followed the counsel to pray my way through the meeting. I felt more promptings from the Lord today than I've felt in a very long time.'

"Fifth, this year we have called special extended ward council meetings as part of ward conferences, and have used them to teach ward leaders how to teach by the Spirit in one-on-one teaching opportunities such as stewardship interviews, monthly home teaching and visiting teaching interviews, and regular interviews with classroom teachers as part of the new emphasis on teaching. It's too early to see many results from this, but we have already heard from a couple of sisters about what a blessing it has been to actually feel love and the Spirit in contacts with Relief Society leaders, instead of a 'How many did you visit this month?' phone call.

"I sincerely thank the Lord for what we've learned about teaching by the Spirit from you and others. We have so very far to go, and I know I'm miles behind where I need to be, but I count myself the most blessed man on earth to be learning these lessons and seeing some of the wonderful miraculous consequences of this simple principle."

What a powerful testimony from a local priesthood leader who is trying to teach by the Spirit in his stake—and from those who are humbly and diligently following his lead.

Another stake president wrote these comments:

"When an Area Authority Seventy came to our stake recently, he talked about how the Brethren are increasingly seeking to speak by the Spirit without a prior agenda for what they are going to say. I have never felt comfortable with that approach for myself, but then I saw this brother do it, and I saw you do it at our meeting the other night. I then decided that I was going to try it myself.

"I gave a talk at a priesthood leadership meeting last Sunday, and I don't think I have ever had so many compliments on any talk I have ever given before. I had nothing written down. I had a few ideas in my mind, and let the Spirit direct my thoughts. What a great blessing it was!

"Shortly after that, I spoke in a ward conference. The same thing occurred, and people came up and thanked me for what I had said.

"Tonight we had a Young Women's Recognition Night, and again I followed this approach. One sister said afterward, 'President Jones, I would love to hear you speak all night because you speak with the Spirit.'

"I have never considered myself a good speaker, and I know that the Lord is doing the speaking when I put myself in his hands and let him guide my thoughts.

"Because of these small successes, I am going to take a major leap of faith in August and speak at stake conference without a formally written talk and without any notes."

I hope no one will take from this chapter that you shouldn't ever use an outline or notes when you give a talk. But I also hope that you'll seek to be moving more in that direction. And some of you could do it right now, if you would only try it. If each of us will trust in the Lord, relying more fully on his Spirit in our teaching, we will find that he will help us more than we know—and we will see his hand blessing our lives and the lives of those we are teaching.

QUESTIONS TO PONDER

1. What suggestions do you find in this chapter regarding your personal preparation before standing to speak? Why are they so important?

_____

_____

_____

2. Why is it difficult for many of us to trust the Lord sufficiently to "speak in the very moment"?

_____

_____

_____

3. What are some ways you could increase your love for the people you are about to teach?

_____

_____

_____

4. What could you do to better discern the actual, current needs of the people you are about to teach?

_____

_____

_____

5. Why is *feeling* so important in teaching?

_____

_____

_____

6. What is the relationship between the presence of the Spirit and outward manifestations of emotional feelings?

_____

_____

_____

7. How can you better teach so people will apply the truths being taught?

_____

_____

_____

CHAPTER 4

PREPARING YOURSELF
AS THE MESSENGER

When we speak of preparing to teach a lesson or give a talk, we often think of preparing material—reading a lesson manual, reviewing scriptures, thinking of stories to include. But when we're teaching by the Spirit, preparing our hearts is far more important than preparing the actual material we will be presenting. This is not easier; it is much harder. But this kind of preparation is infinitely more rewarding.

Remember: if your focus is principally on preparing the lesson, you probably are out of focus. But if you prepare yourself, you can receive the kind of blessing the Lord spoke of to William Law:

> And he shall receive of my Spirit, even the Comforter, which shall manifest unto him the truth of all things, and shall give him, in the very hour, what he shall say. (D&C 124:97.)

As a result of my experience as a newly returned missionary (see the account in the previous chapter), I have almost never written down talks, as I indicated earlier. Sometimes I've written down a few ideas, thoughts, stories, examples, illustrations, and some humor I might use, but it's been very loosely laid out on a sheet of paper. One would not be able to stand and read a talk from my notes. It's been my experience that when we stand to speak, the Lord will truly speak to us in the very moment and help us know what to say.

I have always believed what the Lord told his apostles:

> Behold, I send you forth as sheep in the midst of wolves: be ye therefore wise as serpents, and harmless as doves. But beware of men: for they will deliver you up to the councils, and they will scourge you in their synagogues; and ye shall be brought before governors and kings for my sake, for a testimony against them and the Gentiles. But when they deliver you up, take no thought how or what ye shall speak: for it shall be given you in that same hour what ye shall speak. For it is not ye that speak, but the Spirit of your Father which speaketh in you. (Matthew 10:16–20.)

Thus, through the years I have stood up and it seemed as though the Spirit would just come in the moment. I would try to speak to what I was feeling. Sometimes the Lord would speak to me through individuals who asked a question or shared something in a meeting, which would give me an impression about what I might do to help someone in the audience.

That kind of approach has worked well in such settings as addressing missionaries, stake conferences, youth meetings, and so forth. When I have had to write out a talk for general conference, however, or a talk that needs to be translated, it's been extremely difficult for me to write out the talk beforehand. This is not to imply that we cannot be guided by the Spirit in writing notes or even a talk beforehand. The Spirit can work with each of us in different ways, according to our needs and circumstances.

APPLYING THE PRINCIPLES IN A NEW SETTING

Even though I have understood how to speak without notes, there is one setting that has puzzled me through the years regarding speaking better by the Spirit. That is when I'm with one of the presiding Brethren, and I am called upon to speak from five to thirty minutes in a stake or regional meeting, instead of the one- to two-hour assignments General Authorities usually have.

For example, in regional conferences I might be called on to speak for fifteen to twenty minutes. How do you treat a subject in that time frame when you are used to having two to three times that amount of time? Is there time to tell a story or use an illustration? If you do, will it use up most of the time? When you start a story, you often don't know if it will take two minutes or ten, so it becomes more difficult to stay in the time frame, to know how to teach the way one is accustomed to teaching.

In addition, in most settings where it's possible, I always involve the people. You can't do that when giving a fifteen- to twenty-minute talk in a regional or general conference where hundreds or thousands may be present. This challenge has caused me some frustration.

There are, of course, added concerns when you are with one of the presiding Brethren. You want your message to fit with the spirit of what he desires and to be in unity with what he may speak about. But you also need to have pure enough motives to not be flustered by an improper desire to please the presiding elder or to do well in his sight, instead of focusing on the Lord and the people. All of those feelings have sometimes made it difficult to prepare for a regional conference.

The result is that I began to outline some of the talks and maybe practice them a few times to be sure that I was in the time limit. But when these talks were delivered, time and again they seemed not to be totally me. They seemed to be somewhat stilted and narrow. They weren't spontaneous. They didn't relate as much to the people as when I speak without a script.

Thus I ended up feeling somewhat frustrated about those kinds of talks, not knowing exactly what to do.

Then came a change. I attended another regional conference with one of the senior Brethren of the Quorum of the Twelve. As the conference approached, those same feelings returned—feelings of fear, frustration, anxiety, and wondering, "Why can't I be settled in this kind of teaching setting when I'm so settled in all the rest?"

In praying about it, I felt the Lord wanted me to follow more closely what I've taught for so many years: to not outline a talk, to not determine exactly what I would do beforehand, to not time a talk to see how long it took. I determined to leave all that in the hands of the Lord. I would write down a few ideas that I wanted to convey, maybe a story or illustration that might work, but then leave it very flexible and do my best to speak in the very moment. I would be prayerful that the Lord would help me monitor the time to not speak longer than I was invited to speak.

In other words, I would prepare myself and then would leave the delivery of the talk to the Lord. (Some might feel to take a different approach to speaking and teaching—some might correctly feel that they should write out an outline or even a talk. If we feel to do so, we should seek the Spirit in the preparation—and then be very careful in presenting the material so we are open to impressions that may come "in the moment" that might take us in a very different direction from what we have prepared. I would hope each of us would learn how the Lord desires to work with us in different circumstances.)

It was interesting to me that when we met with the stake presidents prior to the regional conference, the member of the Twelve asked some very penetrating questions of these brethren regarding their stewardships. He gathered some wonderful intelligence about what the presidents were feeling themselves, what their families were facing, and especially what they felt the stake members were facing.

Some of the key problems he asked about were with respect to adults, to youth, to the commandments, to the environment in which they were living, their employment, finances, and so forth. As that information and those feelings were conveyed, it became evident what the Lord would have us do in our talks to try to help them resolve some of their problems.

I really felt the Spirit teaching me, and the member of the Twelve as well, through these brethren who knew the needs of their stake members. I tried to be very prayerful about it. When it was my turn to speak, I did stand up and do as I have typically done in other settings, that is, speak to what I felt, being more flexible, more open to the impressions of the Spirit, and less structured.

It was amazing to see the increase in the Spirit of the Lord that seemed to accompany me in those subsequent teaching settings. It isn't that it wasn't good before, because the Spirit was in what was being taught previously, but in doing it in this manner, the Spirit of the Lord was increased many times over.

The teachings were felt more deeply by the people. It was specific to their particular needs and was received as something that would help them resolve their problems. They knew it. They felt it, and they felt the Spirit of the Lord come upon them and commit them to go forth and do better.

This wonderful member of the Twelve followed the same process. I watched him truly teach by the Spirit and accomplish what we were both attempting to do. It was evident that he was guided by the Spirit. His talks were powerful and truly reached the hearts of the people.

We were both greatly pleased afterward that the Lord had blessed us in uniting our messages, tying them together, and delivering them through his Spirit. It had great impact upon the people, more than I had ever seen at any regional conference up to that time.

THE LORD IS ABLE

I bear testimony to the truth and simplicity of these principles. The Lord does know the needs of his people. He also knows you, the teacher, and if you will prepare yourself, he will inspire you to draw upon stories or illustrations or humor to help resolve the needs of your listeners. He can inspire you directly from heaven with things you do not know, and thus teach you in the process as well.

He can touch your heart while you are teaching, and that will cause others to feel the message more fully. He can bless the people with the Holy Ghost so they will leave the meeting committed to better follow Jesus Christ and purify their lives.

All of that comes about as a result of true teaching by the Spirit. I bear testimony that it works. This is the Lord's kingdom. This is his gospel. These are his teachings. He surely knows how to convey them and is more able to do so as we become more open and flexible and trusting that he will speak through us.

I bear testimony that the simplest soul can do what I have just described. It is not a matter of how much you know. It is a matter of whether or not you are willing to humble yourself and believe that the Lord will speak through you, willing to prepare yourself as an instrument, and then willing to give him that opportunity, despite the feeling of risk to yourself—the risk of failing, of not doing well, of being awkward in your sentence structure, of stumbling over yourself.

If those feelings of risk are replaced with true faith, I testify that the Lord will speak through his servants—men, women, and children—and the message will better reach the hearts of his people.

PREPARING MIND AND HEART

A former member of the Quorums of the Seventy, Elder C. Max Caldwell, had this experience with preparing to teach:

"Some years ago I prepared to teach a class on a subject I felt would be particularly difficult. The night before the scheduled class, I prayed for guidance and then retired, still troubled in my mind. When I awoke, a certain thought was introduced to my mind that I shared with the class later that morning. After the class, a young man spoke with me privately and said, 'The lesson was for me. I now know what I have to do.' Later I learned that he had come to that class as his first contact with the Church in many years. He then proceeded to get his life in order and eventually served a faithful mission. Presently he is experiencing the happiness associated with keeping eternal family covenants" ("Love of Christ," *Ensign*, Nov. 1992, 29–30).

The blessing of this sweet experience came to Elder Caldwell and his class not only because he sought to prepare a lesson, but also because he sought to prepare himself.

The Lord has repeatedly given us counsel on preparing ourselves to teach by his Spirit. "Seek not to declare my word, but first seek to obtain my word," he said, "and then shall your tongue be loosed; then, if you desire, you shall have my Spirit and my word, yea, the power of God unto the convincing of men" (D&C 11:21).

There is a vital difference between "teaching" and "teaching by the Spirit." When we simply try to teach, we prepare the lesson or the talk. When we seek to teach by the Spirit, we also seek to prepare *ourselves*. This is so important that if someone were to ask me, "What is the single greatest thing you know about teaching?" I would quickly respond that it *must be done by the Spirit*. Then I would add: There is one thing that has a greater effect than anything else on teaching and learning by the Spirit, and that is to prepare ourselves by placing our hearts in tune with the Lord, which we accomplish largely through prayer.

Latter-day apostles give us additional counsel on preparing ourselves to teach. Elder Dallin H. Oaks has written:

"Teaching by the Spirit requires first that we keep the commandments and be clean before God so his Spirit can dwell in our personal temples. . . .

"We must, therefore, cleanse ourselves by repentance, by confession when necessary, and by avoiding impure actions and thoughts. . . .

"[We also] obtain the Spirit by reading the scriptures or reading or listening to the talks of inspired leaders" ("Teaching and Learning by the Spirit," *Ensign*, Mar. 1997, 9).

Elder Jeffrey R. Holland has taught that "most people don't come to church looking merely for a few new gospel facts or to see old friends, though all of that is important. They come seeking a spiritual experience. They want peace. They want their faith fortified and their hope renewed. They want, in short, to be nourished by the good word of God, to be strengthened by the powers of heaven. Those of us who are called upon to speak or teach or lead have an obligation to help provide that, as best we possibly can. We can only do that if we ourselves are striving to know God, if we ourselves are continually seeking the light of His Only Begotten Son. Then, if our hearts are right, if we are as clean as we can be, if we have prayed and wept and prepared and worried until we don't know what more we can do, God can say to us as He did to Alma and the sons of Mosiah: 'Lift up thy head and rejoice. . . . I will give unto you success.' (Alma 8:15; 26:27.)" ("'A Teacher Come from God,'" *Ensign*, May 1998, 26).

As a teacher you must learn how to prepare your own heart to *receive* the word of the Lord. If you will continually do that you will also then know how to prepare the hearts of those you teach. The Lord reiterates frequently in the scriptures the concept of *preparing the way*. That preparation seems to be assisted by the Lord, by his angels, by leaders, and by each of us, ourselves, as we come to understand how to do it.

AGENTS IN THE PREPARATION PROCESS

The Lord Will Sometimes Act Directly to Help Prepare Our Hearts

And there was no inequality among them; the Lord did pour out his Spirit on all the face of the land to prepare the minds of the children of men, or to prepare their hearts to receive the word which should be taught among them at the time of his coming. (Alma 16:16.)

Sometimes the Lord Will Send Angels to Help in the Preparation Process

For behold, angels are declaring it unto many at this time in our land; and this is for the purpose of preparing the hearts of the children of men to receive his word at the time of his coming in his glory. (Alma 13:24.)

And the office of their ministry is to call men unto repentance, and to fulfil and to do the work of the covenants of the Father, which he hath made unto the children of men, to prepare the way among the children of men, by declaring the word of Christ unto the chosen vessels of the Lord, that they may bear testimony of him. (Moroni 7:31.)

Sometimes Our Leaders Are Instrumental in Our Preparation

And now, as the preaching of the word had a great tendency to lead the people to do that which was just—yea, it had had more powerful effect upon the minds of the people than the sword, or anything else, which had happened unto them—therefore Alma thought it was expedient that they should try the virtue of the word of God. (Alma 31:5.)

He hath spoken somewhat unto you to prepare your minds; yea, and he hath exhorted you unto faith and to patience—yea, even that ye would have so much faith as even to plant the word in your hearts, that ye may try the experiment of its goodness. (Alma 34:3–4.)

And it came to pass that I did speak many words unto my brethren, that they were pacified and did humble themselves before the Lord. (1 Nephi 15:20.)

And ye are called to bring to pass the gathering of mine elect; for mine elect hear my voice and harden not their hearts. (D&C 29:7.)

SOME PRINCIPLES OF PERSONAL PREPARATION

We can receive help from others in the process of preparing our hearts to receive and teach by the Spirit. But most of the work of preparation must be done by ourselves. How do we do it? I would suggest that we consider the following principles, which have been drawn from an attempt to understand from the scriptures some of the many different ways the Lord has given us to more fully increase the influence of the Spirit in our teaching.

As you review the principles that are about to be described, please do not feel overburdened by them. One does not have to do all of these things every time. They have been listed here to give you added ways of increasing the Spirit of the Lord in your teaching as you seek and grow through the years. In one sense it is a lifetime labor to be able to fully apply all of these principles.

Don't feel overburdened—but as you read the scriptures

presented here, do seek to understand from the Spirit how you might personally apply the principles being taught.

Preparing Our Hearts through Pondering and Prayer

When the Savior taught in his personal visitation to the Nephites after the resurrection, he told them that he had to leave, but that he would return the next day to teach them further.

> Therefore, go ye unto your homes, and ponder upon the things which I have said, and ask of the Father, in my name, that ye may understand, and prepare your minds for the morrow, and I come unto you again. (3 Nephi 17:3.)

Here we have two of the principles of preparation: to ponder and pray, seeking understanding of the Lord's word.

In our day, the Lord taught anew the principle of seeking understanding through prayer:

> And they shall give heed to that which is written, and pretend to no other revelation; and they shall pray always that I may unfold the same to their understanding. (D&C 32:4.)

Humbling Ourselves

> Be thou humble; and the Lord thy God shall lead thee by the hand, and give thee answer to thy prayers. (D&C 112:10.)

> Let him that is ignorant learn wisdom by humbling himself and calling upon the Lord his God, that his eyes may be opened that he may see, and his ears opened that he may hear; for my Spirit is sent forth into the world to enlighten the humble and contrite. (D&C 136:32–33; see also Ether 12:27.)

Behold, I say unto him, he exalts himself and does not humble himself sufficiently before me; but if he will bow down before me, and humble himself in mighty prayer and faith, in the sincerity of his heart, then will I grant unto him a view of the things which he desires to see. . . .

And now, except he humble himself and acknowledge unto me the things that he has done which are wrong, and covenant with me that he will keep my commandments, and exercise faith in me, behold, I say unto him, he shall have no such views, for I will grant unto him no views of the things of which I have spoken. (D&C 5:24, 28.)

It is evident that the attribute of humility is fundamental in learning anything from the Lord. The Lord will enlighten the humble. The Lord will answer the prayers of the humble. The Lord will open the eyes and ears of the humble and in the process make them strong.

If you truly desire to speak by the Spirit, each time you approach such an assignment do your very best to humble yourself and trust that the Lord will speak through the humble man or woman.

Acknowledging Our Unworthiness before God

Do not say: O God, I thank thee that we are better than our brethren; but rather say: O Lord, forgive my unworthiness, and remember my brethren in mercy—yea, acknowledge your unworthiness before God at all times. (Alma 38:14.)

And it came to pass that the Lord said unto me: . . . because thou hast seen thy weakness thou shalt be made strong, even unto the sitting down in the place which I have prepared in the mansions of my Father. (Ether 12:37; see also Luke 18:13–14; Romans 12:3.)

One way of humbling ourselves is to remember our unworthiness before the Lord. If we count our sins and recognize them, we will tend to humble ourselves and thus invite the Spirit of the Lord more fully into our lives.

Repenting and Keeping the Commandments, Seeking to Retain a Remission of Our Sins

Let us look at how the Lord describes a repentant soul. We find that if we are repentant, we will be given many of the gifts of the Spirit and will be filled with the fruits of the Spirit, namely love, hope, peace, and so forth.

> And the first fruits of repentance is baptism; and baptism cometh by faith unto the fulfilling the commandments; and the fulfilling the commandments bringeth remission of sins; and the remission of sins bringeth meekness, and lowliness of heart; and because of meekness and lowliness of heart cometh the visitation of the Holy Ghost, which Comforter filleth with hope and perfect love, which love endureth by diligence unto prayer, until the end shall come, when all the saints shall dwell with God. (Moroni 8:25–26; see also Mosiah 4:11–12, 26; Alma 26:21–22.)

If we desire to increase the intensity of the Spirit, we must do our best to keep the commandments of the Lord, thereby retaining a remission of our sins, which will invite the Holy Ghost to come and visit us and become our constant companion.

Alma spoke to his son, Corianton, about the attitudes and feelings that accompany a repentant heart:

> And now, my son, I desire that ye should let these things trouble you no more, and only let your sins trouble you, with that trouble which shall bring you down unto repentance. O my son, I desire that ye should deny the justice of God no more. Do not endeavor to excuse yourself in the least point because of your sins, by denying the justice of God; but do you let the justice of God, and his mercy, and his long-suffering have full sway in your heart;

and let it bring you down to the dust in humility. (Alma 42:29–30.)

Learning to Increase the Spirit's Intensity

Pray always, and I will pour out my Spirit upon you, and great shall be your blessing—yea, even more than if you should obtain treasures of earth and corruptibleness to the extent thereof. (D&C 19:38.)

Again I say, hearken ye elders of my church, whom I have appointed: Ye are not sent forth to be taught, but to teach the children of men the things which I have put into your hands by the power of my Spirit; and ye are to be taught from on high. Sanctify yourselves and ye shall be endowed with power, that ye may give even as I have spoken. (D&C 43:15–16.)

And now I, Nephi, cannot write all the things which were taught among my people; neither am I mighty in writing, like unto speaking; for when a man speaketh by the power of the Holy Ghost the power of the Holy Ghost carrieth it unto the hearts of the children of men. (2 Nephi 33:1.)

If we desire to teach by the Spirit of the Lord, we must work at having increased amounts of the Spirit of the Lord with us. That will come if we pray for it and truly try to sanctify ourselves. We must believe that the Spirit will be given us, and that it will be conveyed by the power of our testimony to others.

Seeking to Be Filled with Love

And faith, hope, charity and love, with an eye single to the glory of God, qualify him for the work. (D&C 4:5.)

But charity is the pure love of Christ, and it endureth forever. . . . Wherefore, my beloved brethren, pray unto the Father with all the energy of heart, that ye may be filled with this love, which he hath bestowed upon all who are true followers of his Son, Jesus Christ. (Moroni 7:47–48.)

For if we had not come up out of the land of Zarahemla, these our dearly beloved brethren, who have so dearly beloved us, would still have been racked with hatred against us, yea, and they would also have been strangers to God. . . .

Behold, how many thousands of our brethren has he loosed from the pains of hell; and they are brought to sing redeeming love, and this because of the power of his word which is in us, therefore have we not great reason to rejoice? . . .

Therefore, let us glory, yea, we will glory in the Lord; yea, we will rejoice, for our joy is full; yea, we will praise our God forever. Behold, who can glory too much in the Lord? Yea, who can say too much of his great power, and of his mercy, and of his long-suffering towards the children of men? Behold, I say unto you, I cannot say the smallest part which I feel. (Alma 26:9, 13, 16.)

Love. Increased amounts of love for God and for the people bring increased amounts of the Spirit. In fact, the degree to which you truly love the people and they feel the love of you as their teacher dictates in large measure how much of the Spirit will be there to allow you to teach by the Spirit.

We are reminded in the scriptures that we must pray with all the energy of our heart to have this love, and that it is one of the qualifications for the work.

Controlling Our Thoughts and Bridling Our Passions

But this much I can tell you, that if ye do not watch yourselves, and your thoughts, and your words, and your deeds, and observe the commandments of God, and continue in the faith of what ye have heard concerning the coming of our Lord, even unto the end of your lives, ye must perish. And now, O man, remember, and perish not. (Mosiah 4:30.)

Use boldness, but not overbearance; and also see that ye bridle all your passions, that ye may be filled with love; see that ye refrain from idleness. (Alma 38:12.)

We must truly guard our thoughts to be sure we speak the thoughts of the Lord and not our own thoughts. If we will do that, the Lord will give us utterance and speak through us. We must control our thoughts and our passions, and then we will be filled with the love of God.

Searching and Using the Scriptures

Seek not to declare my word, but first seek to obtain my word, and then shall your tongue be loosed; then, if you desire, you shall have my Spirit and my word, yea, the power of God unto the convincing of men.

But now hold your peace; study my word which hath gone forth among the children of men, . . . until you have obtained all which I shall grant unto the children of men in this generation, and then shall all things be added thereto. (D&C 11:21–22.)

And now, as the preaching of the word had a great tendency to lead the people to do that which was just— yea, it had had more powerful effect upon the minds of the people than the sword, or anything else, which had happened unto them—therefore Alma thought it was expedient that they should try the virtue of the word of God. (Alma 31:5; see also 2 Nephi 32:3; D&C 1:37.)

There are probably few things that will increase our ability to speak by the Spirit as much as learning, understanding, and even memorizing some of the scriptures. When we allow the Lord to speak by quoting or reading the Lord's answers to the various questions of life, we will find there is much greater power in our teaching. The scriptures will allow us to speak for the Lord clearly and with authority. To do so, we must search them and learn what the Lord has said.

Fasting with a Purpose

If we truly desire to increase the Spirit in our teaching, fasting is one of the best ways to do it. Fasting has the tendency to humble us and cause us to set aside the temporal world and our temporal desires and to focus on that which is spiritual. It will draw us closer to God and thus allow us to speak by the Spirit more fully.

> They had given themselves to much prayer, and fasting; therefore they had the spirit of prophecy, and the spirit of revelation, and when they taught, they taught with power and authority of God. (Alma 17:3.)

> Do ye not suppose that I know of these things myself? Behold, I testify unto you that I do know that these things whereof I have spoken are true. And how do ye suppose that I know of their surety? Behold, I say unto you they are made known unto me by the Holy Spirit of God. Behold, I have fasted and prayed many days that I might know these things of myself. And now I do know of myself that they are true; for the Lord God hath made them manifest unto me by his Holy Spirit; and this is the spirit of revelation which is in me. (Alma 5:45–46.)

Seeking the Will of the Lord

> And the Holy Ghost giveth authority that I should speak these things, and deny them not. (1 Nephi 10:22.)

> He that asketh in the Spirit asketh according to the will of God; wherefore it is done even as he asketh. (D&C 46:30; see also Helaman 10:4–5.)

> Wherefore, as ye are agents, ye are on the Lord's errand; and whatever ye do according to the will of the Lord is the Lord's business. (D&C 64:29.)

If we will truly seek to have the Spirit of the Lord, we will be able to speak according to the will of the Lord, and thus that which we say will come to pass. Seeking diligently to submit yourself always to the Lord's will and setting aside your own agenda will invite increased amounts of the Spirit to be with you.

Earnestly Seeking to Bless the People

There is nothing quite like truly loving the people and seeking their best interest for inviting additional portions of the Spirit of the Lord. If we will do as indicated in the following scriptures, seeking out the needs of the people, that will increase our ability to speak by the Spirit. Thus, each time you are preparing to speak, truly ponder beforehand what the needs of the people might be—the situation they find themselves in, circumstances in their employment, their financial strengths or weaknesses, challenges in Church callings, challenges in their families, or the challenge of being single.

If you will prayerfully consider these things, you will find the Spirit will more fully guide you in your preparation. Even while you are delivering your talk or lesson, if you will be sensitive to the needs of the people at the moment, you will find an increase in the influence of the Spirit guiding you.

> My father, Lehi, as he went forth prayed unto the Lord, yea, even with all his heart, in behalf of his people. (1 Nephi 1:5.)

> Alma labored much in the spirit, wrestling with God in mighty prayer, that he would pour out his Spirit upon the people who were in the city; that he would also grant that he might baptize them unto repentance. (Alma 8:10.)

I am desirous for the welfare of your souls. Yea, mine anxiety is great for you; and ye yourselves know that it ever has been. For I have exhorted you with all diligence. (2 Nephi 6:3.)

Ye yourselves know that I have hitherto been diligent in the office of my calling; but I this day am weighed down with much more desire and anxiety for the welfare of your souls than I have hitherto been. (Jacob 2:3.)

Seeking to Discern the People's Needs

For because of faith and great anxiety, it truly had been made manifest unto us concerning our people, what things should happen unto them. (Jacob 1:5.)

Now they knew not that Amulek could know of their designs. But it came to pass as they began to question him, he perceived their thoughts. (Alma 10:17.)

Zeezrom . . . was convinced more and more of the power of God; and he was also convinced that Alma and Amulek had a knowledge of him, for he was convinced that they knew the thoughts and intents of his heart; for power was given unto them that they might know of these things according to the spirit of prophecy. (Alma 12:7.)

And to others the discerning of spirits. (D&C 46:23.)

If we spend our time preparing the material of a talk or a lesson, but don't devote any effort to preparing ourselves, we are sacrificing the thing of greater importance to do the thing of lesser importance. Yes, it is important that we thoughtfully and prayerfully review the material of a talk or lesson. But it is much more important to seek to prepare our hearts to receive the Spirit, that we may then be true instruments for the Lord.

How then can we prepare our hearts to receive and teach by the Spirit? The scriptures we have reviewed give us several key principles. To prepare ourselves we can:

1. Prepare our hearts through pondering and prayer.
2. Humble ourselves.
3. Acknowledge our unworthiness before God.
4. Repent and keep the commandments, seeking to retain a remission of our sins.
5. Learn to increase the Spirit's intensity.
6. Seek to be filled with love.
7. Control our thoughts and bridle our passions.
8. Search and use the scriptures.
9. Fast with a purpose.
10. Seek the will of the Lord.
11. Earnestly seek to bless the people.
12. Seek to discern the people's needs.

Again, I don't believe that the Lord requires us to do all of these things at once. We grow in our teaching and in our preparation little by little, step by step. And if this seems to be a long list, perhaps we could condense it down to the most essential elements: to receive the Spirit in our teaching, we need to desire that Spirit, be worthy, and seek it through prayer, with humble hearts.

Humility in this process cannot be overemphasized. The story is told of an overconfident speaker who approached the pulpit well prepared but feeling no need for the help of the Lord. Because he had not sought the Spirit and because he was not humble, his talk did not go very well and he was embarrassed. Afterward, an older fellow said to him, "If you would have come up the way you went down, you could have come down the way you went up."

We must never begin to think that we understand the scriptures—or a given doctrine—so well that we can now be the "teacher." As soon as we begin to think that we're pretty good—without the help of the Lord—the Spirit will begin to withdraw, and we will indeed begin to be left on our own.

Would these words not apply to us as well as to non-believers:

> Wo be unto him that shall say: We have received the word of God, and we need no more of the word of God, for we have enough! For behold, thus saith the Lord God: I will give unto the children of men line upon line, precept upon precept, here a little and there a little; and blessed are those who hearken unto my precepts, and lend an ear unto my counsel, for they shall learn wisdom; for unto him that receiveth I will give more; and from them that shall say, We have enough, from them shall be taken away even that which they have. (2 Nephi 28:29–31.)

If we are prideful in our teaching, the Lord will take away our gifts and powers. But on the other hand, if we will humble ourselves and pray consistently to the Lord, he will be with us in our lives and in our teaching. He will open our eyes that we may see and our ears that we may hear. He will help us to be prepared in our hearts, so the Spirit will attend us in all we do. I bear witness that this is true.

Perhaps the following chart summarizes the importance of not only preparing to speak, but of preparing *ourselves*.

LEVELS OF EFFECTIVE TEACHING

A GOOD TEACHER SHOULD	AN INSPIRED TEACHER MUST
use participation use workshops follow-up with students tell personal experiences use eye contact be well prepared show concern for the student know the students use visual aids use the scriptures study, know, and use materials well praise the students	be in constant contact with the Lord be full of love be filled with faith live the teachings be humble be patient, tolerant, temperate be nourished by the Spirit testify be enthusiastic teach the doctrine teach with the Spirit be an example
The mechanics—the "branches": This approach describes the techniques of a good teacher—what he does. This approach centers on materials and techniques, and expects students to learn from what the teacher tells or teaches them. The objective with this approach is for the teacher to do these things to the learner so he will learn. With this approach, the teacher *gives* the result—gives "learning or information." The student may be made weaker or dependent, while the teacher does most of the work and striving. With this approach, the objective is to *tell* the student.	**The Spirit—the "root":** This approach describes the teacher, the person himself. This approach causes the teacher to turn the students to the Lord and to learn how to learn from *Him*. The teacher's role is to exemplify in his soul the way a good teacher lives. The student is helped to be self-motivated and to learn from God. The objective in this approach is for the student to rely on the Lord and learn from him. With this approach, the teacher is involved in giving overall direction, getting the student to give of self and be involved. The teacher does less "traditional teaching." The student does the work, striving, and searching. With this approach, the objective is to create a desire and need in the student to search things out for himself.

We should all seek to do those things that good, effective teachers do. But, even more importantly, we should all seek to teach by the Spirit! The best teacher will seek to excel in the things in both columns—but he or she will give primary emphasis to the items found in column 2.

PREPARATION IN ACTION

Let me share with you two experiences that show some of these principles in action. The first experience was related to me by a stake president. He wrote:

"Our stake Relief Society president recently called a special meeting of all ward Relief Society presidents to discuss a major procedural change that earlier feedback had indicated was not going to be well accepted. She was terrified to face all those sisters, even though she had received her own witness that the change was the will of the Lord. We counseled her, 'Sister, you don't have to do this yourself. Just prepare the messenger and let the Spirit do the rest.'

"She fasted, prayed, went to the temple, and received a priesthood blessing from her husband. When she arrived at the dreaded meeting she discovered that the Spirit had already been at work. The change was received with gratitude, and the sisters unanimously made the commitment without one single word of opposition or concern. Some of the most tender and positive feelings came from those who had earlier expressed opposition. The Lord *still* is the Master Teacher."

The second experience happened in my own home, with one of my sons. (I'll call him John.) One night John came to me and asked me what he should teach the lesson on in the priests quorum the next Sunday. The teacher had been having some of the priests teach the lessons, and John had been concerned about what topic he ought to teach. He was very restless and uneasy and anything but peaceful.

He pressed me to give him some ideas. I simply said, "John, what you ought to talk about in the priests quorum is what the Lord would want you to talk about, and one of the best ways to find that out is to truly ponder the needs of the young men in your quorum. What do they really need? What are some of the things they're not doing quite right? You ponder what their needs are and pray to the Lord and ask him what he would have you talk about, and you will find out."

In about fifteen to twenty minutes, John reappeared and I could tell that he was full of peace. I asked him what he was going to do, and he said, "I feel very strongly that I should talk about how the priests treat their families; how they could love them more, obey them, and not speak badly of their parents."

I then explained to John the importance of teaching by the Spirit, that it was more important to teach by the Spirit than give content to the people, even though they need both. Earlier, he had memorized some suggestions I had given to him for inviting the Spirit of the Lord into a meeting. He knew them all and prepared to teach with them. (We will talk about those principles in the next chapter.)

It was evident now that the Lord had directed him and he knew it. In our scripture reading the next morning, we discussed John's experience. We confirmed to him that when you are going to give a talk, a clear feeling that the Lord would have you deliver a message to the people gives you a much stronger faith in the Lord and in yourself to be able to deliver the message. The Spirit seems to come with more intensity or power. It was a good learning experience for John and for all of us in the family.

On the following Sunday, two adult men came up to me and told me of the wonderful impact of John's lesson on all the priests. They said he shared some tears, and his testimony really reached the hearts of the young men in the quorum meeting. One of the priests who lives near us sought me out to tell me that John had borne such a powerful testimony that it helped him truly change some things in his life.

It's amazing how a young man can bear witness and have the Spirit of the Lord respond so quickly. I am confident that the Lord blessed John to succeed in this endeavor.

John felt that one of the major reasons the Spirit was

present throughout his class was that he had invited the Spirit to be there by using some of the suggestions we will treat in the next chapter. Afterward he seemed very confident that they would work for him, as well as for others who use those principles. He had prepared himself through prayer, study, and worthiness. He had prepared by seeking to know the needs of his priests and the will of the Lord. And they all had had a great experience as a result of John's preparation.

QUESTIONS TO PONDER

1. How can you both prepare the material to be taught and at the same time maintain a major emphasis on preparing yourself so you can speak by the Spirit?

_____

_____

_____

2. Why does the Spirit seem to come to a person more freely in an unstructured teaching setting?

_____

_____

_____

3. How can you better apply some of the principles of personal preparation discussed in this chapter?

_____

_____

_____

4. Can a person really assist in increasing the intensity of the Spirit felt in a teaching situation?

_____

_____

_____

CHAPTER 5

INVITING THE SPIRIT
INTO OUR TEACHING

As you may know, the Church has traditionally had a real challenge reactivating many of the members who have turned from the Lord and become less-active. In some ways it has seemed like an impossible task. Some years ago when I was serving in California the Church had some great success with activation. We tried to teach local leaders there to go boldly in the name of the Lord into the homes of the less-active members. These were not to be just social or chit-chat visits, but the leaders, in great love and with the Spirit of the Lord, were to have a spiritual experience with the members, call them to repentance, and begin to bring them back to Christ. In one year there were about 15,000 children, youth, and adults who came back into the Church—all because good brothers and sisters were going into their homes, teaching the doctrine, bearing witness and, sometimes, even singing a hymn.

In one meeting a few years ago, we had brought a group of mission presidents and Regional Representatives together. I said, "I'm getting weary of hearing talks on reactivation. I would like to see some face-to-face interaction. And we're going to get started this very night by going into their homes." We then gave them about twenty minutes of instruction about how to proceed in their visits. (Part of the instruction included the very things I talk about in this book.) We then prayed together and sent them on their way.

I suggested they take a hymnbook with them, as they might be impressed to sing. One priesthood leader began to walk out without his hymnbook, and I said, "Hey, wait. You forgot your book."

He said, "Listen, Brother Cook. With all due respect, I will do six of the seven things you suggested. But one of them I will not do and that is sing. I have a terrible voice and I can't do it."

I said, "Well, I know you're not planning on singing, but what if the Lord is planning on your doing it anyway? You'd better take your book."

He mumbled a bit and then took the book. But as he did so, he said in his heart, as he reported to us later, "I'll never sing, not for anybody."

His testimony to us later that evening was very interesting. He said, "We got into the house of a less-active member, a man about sixty years old, with his wife and less-active son. We prayed with them. I read the scriptures. I bore my testimony. But our visit just wasn't going anywhere. This hard-hearted man was just sitting there resisting us." He continued, "I was praying, 'Father, what shall we do? How can we humble this man before Thee so that we can teach him with the Spirit?' and the next thing I knew my young companion stood up in that living room and said, 'My companion and I are going to sing to you.'" The priesthood leader said, "I couldn't believe what I had heard." But they stood up to sing anyway. He said, "I probably selfishly picked the shortest song in the hymnbook— 'As I Have Loved You.'" He thought he could get through that one.

These two men, one about forty and the other about sixty— two companions who had never sung to an audience before in their lives—stood up in front of this older less-active fellow, his wife, and his son. They started singing, "*As I have loved you, love one another. This new commandment . . ."* They got about halfway through the song and this less-active fellow started weeping. They then bore testimony and taught him some basic principles about how to pray. He sat there with tears running down his cheeks, totally humbled.

The priesthood leader who couldn't sing reported to all of us later, "I know I have a terrible voice, but my voice tonight was as the voice of an angel."

I added, "You may just be right."

I learned shortly thereafter that the man they had visited had started to pay a full tithing and had begun to attend some of his sacrament meetings and ward socials, due at least in part to someone who knew how to use music to humble the hearts of the people.

As a result of the activation efforts of that one night, about forty-five people were activated and thirty-eight or thirty-nine have gone through the temple.

Singing hymns is just one way to invite the Spirit into our teaching. (And we'll talk more about singing hymns later in this chapter.) There are other powerful ways we can invite the Spirit to join us immediately, to support and help us in our teaching effort.

It has been said that you cannot force spiritual things. Certainly the Spirit of the Lord is not just our servant, simply waiting to do our bidding. But at the same time the Spirit is eager to be with us, to help us, to bless us. If we will create an environment for the Spirit in our own hearts and in the teaching setting, that Spirit will come and all present who will be open to it will be blessed.

How can a teacher in Relief Society or a priesthood quorum help to invite the Spirit into that meeting? How can a priesthood leader more fully bring the Spirit into an interview? What can a husband do to improve the spirit when his wife is upset and they need to talk about serious concerns in their marriage?

Maybe your father is less active and you haven't been able to reach him. What do you do to try to reach him with the Spirit? Suppose you're a visiting teacher to a lady who is somewhat hard-hearted. What can you do to bless her through the Spirit?

I would like to share seven suggestions of things we can do that can help to bring the Spirit into a meeting or interview or teaching situation—and, if we're worthy and our hearts are humble, the response will be immediate. I believe the Spirit will respond to our honest efforts through prayer, using scriptures, testimony, the singing of hymns, expressing love and gratitude to God and man, sharing spiritual experiences, and giving priesthood blessings. (Most of these ideas are discussed in the excellent Church teaching manual, *Teaching, No Greater Call: A Resource Guide for Gospel Teaching*. These suggestions have also been mentioned in some of my other writings, but due to their importance as they relate to teaching by the Spirit, let us expand on them here, with this subject in mind.)

INVITE THE SPIRIT THROUGH PRAYER

One of the most important things we can do to receive the Spirit is to pray fervently for it. As the scriptures say, the Spirit will be given to us "*by the prayer of faith*" (D&C 42:14). The Lord here is not simply telling us to pray in faith. We should also explicitly pray that the Spirit will be with us in our lives and in our teaching.

In addition to praying before the meeting (or other teaching experience) that the Spirit will be with us, we also need to pray at the very moment of the teaching. We should pray our way through the visit, pray our way through the interview, pray our way through the meeting. We need to open our hearts and ask the Lord for his help, having a spirit and attitude of seeking his counsel. Over the years I've had many of my prayers answered at the very moment when I needed help, during the very meeting when I was teaching. And I've learned that if you'll be specific about what you want and pray while you're in the meeting, you'll be amazed at some of the answers that come.

Once I was teaching a group of priesthood leaders. I was probably fifteen minutes into my presentation, and even though I had good material and there was a good spirit there, somehow I felt that something was not right. I felt uneasy, but when you're teaching in front of a group the tendency is to just keep going. But somehow I knew that I was giving them a "B" message when the Lord wanted them to receive an "A" message.

I remember stopping for a moment and praying, "Please, Heavenly Father, help me. What should I do?" After the prayer I said, "I just feel impressed that there are a couple of people here who need to bear a testimony. I invite you to come up." Then I stopped. They all looked at me with a little bit of shock. Then two men came up. They both delivered a message straight from the heart. What they said needed to be said *right then*, and it was clearly evident that they were providing the missing piece in my presentation. Those testimonies took us in quite a different direction from where we had been headed.

The Lord, in his majesty, blessed us. Perhaps he had tried to communicate with me before the meeting, giving me a different direction—and I just didn't hear. Or perhaps he wanted us in the meeting to hear those testimonies delivered from the heart. Whatever his purpose, he heard my prayers and helped me to turn that meeting in the direction he wanted.

Those who are listening should also be praying through a meeting. Not infrequently during a meeting we will have an impression from the Lord that has absolutely nothing to do with the speaker. Perhaps the thought comes, "You should go see Mary as soon as this meeting's over," or "Your boy is having difficulty in this area—here's an idea of what to do." Even though the impression may have nothing to do with the subject of the talk or lesson, we can receive such guidance from the Lord when we are humble, praying, asking for help. President Boyd K. Packer likes to say, "Revelation comes to us in conclusions." If you are watching for that and trying to prepare your heart to receive it, believing you will, then you will.

If you are teaching or speaking and you do not feel the Spirit, it may be necessary for you to say so. Solicit the support of the members to make a greater effort to receive the Spirit of the Lord, praying in their hearts, so that the meeting will be the Lord's meeting. I remember I once attended with a member of the Twelve a meeting that was not going very well. This good brother said, "I take the blame on myself for not having done my part to bring the Spirit into this meeting. Will you help me to change the situation?"

There is also great power in praying *with* someone else. Some members have children with whom they are struggling. Some teachers have students who are struggling. If it were appropriate for a teacher to kneel in prayer with her student, that could have a much greater impact by far than if the teacher simply talked to the student. Students need to see prayer in action. They need to feel it. And then the Spirit will have a greater opening to come into their hearts.

I think of missionaries who are trying to lead people to conversion. Sometimes missionaries have a tendency to counter objections from the scriptures, to explain, to reason the problem away. Those approaches have their place. But prayer is even more powerful. Suppose an investigator were to give an objection to paying his tithing. The missionary could say, "What did the Lord say about tithing when you asked him? Come on, Brother Brown, let's kneel down and talk to Him." Then the missionary puts Brother Brown into the hands of the Lord, and, as a result, Brother Brown's heart can be changed by the Spirit.

Teachers, leaders, and parents should remember the

example of Aaron with Lamoni's father. After Aaron taught him the truth, Lamoni's father asked how he could come to the blessings of which Aaron had spoken. Aaron directed him to go straight to the Lord: "If thou wilt repent of all thy sins, and will bow down before God, and call on his name in faith, believing that ye shall receive, then shalt thou receive the hope which thou desirest" (Alma 22:16). The king then prayed in deep humility, and the Spirit came (see Alma 22:17–18).

We should never hesitate to invite people to pray, even if we have already started the teaching situation with prayer. For example, if an investigator cannot accept the need for a living prophet, rather than rely on scripture alone for the answer, we can simply invite the person to kneel in prayer and ask God, *right now,* if there is a need. Aaron did not hesitate to ask Lamoni's father to pray in the middle of the "discussion."

When parents have a problem with one of their children, it should be one of their first inclinations to find a private place and pray with him. To those who have that kind of mindset, I would say, "Bless you for humbly recognizing that God is in his heavens. He holds all nations in his hands and is surely capable of helping you." I bear witness that the Lord speaks to those who go to him. He gives them revelation. He can touch the heart of a child or a student or someone else who is not responding, if they will allow his gentle touch. But we can't do those things without him. Prayer can open the door to the Spirit in every teaching situation.

INVITE THE SPIRIT BY USING THE SCRIPTURES

If you want to invite the Spirit of the Lord immediately, use the scriptures. If you're teaching and something is not working very well—either in your Primary class, at home, or even in a ward council meeting—take a few seconds to prepare your mind and humble yourself before you continue. Then pick up the scriptures and start reading, with true feeling and a humble heart. Especially powerful are those passages with which you have had a spiritual experience, and you should particularly consider using those. Pray for your students as you read. As you do so, the Spirit will often come immediately because the scriptures are the Lord's words, and the Spirit will bear witness of the truth of those words if you do your part.

There is great power in teaching from the scriptures. Learn the scriptures and teach from them. They will have "more powerful effect upon the minds of the people than the sword, or anything else" (Alma 31:5). The word of God in scriptures leads people to faith in Jesus Christ, to repentance, and to a change of heart (see Helaman 15:7–8). To know how to use a reference or which one to use, we must rely upon the Lord and what we have personally studied. We can use the scriptures to pacify and humble the heart of one of little faith. As we read in the Book of Mormon:

> And I did rehearse unto them the words of Isaiah. . . . And it came to pass that I did speak many words unto my brethren, that they were pacified and did humble themselves before the Lord. (1 Nephi 15:20; see also 16:4–5.)

A similar concept is expressed in latter-day revelation:

> This is the most expedient in me, that my word should go forth unto the children of men, for the purpose of subduing the hearts of the children of men for your good. (D&C 96:5.)

The scriptures, then, can help to bring a new spirit into a discussion—a spirit wherein those involved can be pacified, humbled, and subdued, more willing to submit themselves to the Lord.

When our children or students ask questions, sometimes we have a tendency to give our own opinions or to say, "Well, I've been around a long time; let me tell you about my experiences."

A much better approach is to say, "You know, John, the Lord answered that very question. Let's read a few verses in Alma 32 and see what we can understand." We can have a great impact upon the souls of men when we use the Lord's words and let the Lord speak for himself to the people when we are teaching.

A couple of years ago I attended a stake conference in southern Utah. As I was shaking hands before the meeting I saw a lady with her head down, reading the scriptures. She looked like she was thirty-five or forty years old. I approached her and kiddingly said, "Well, it looks like you're reading a pretty good book." This wonderful sister looked up at me with tears streaming down her face. I knew then that I should not kid her, that she was having a real spiritual experience. I said, "Good sister, what are you reading about?" And she said, weeping, "Oh, Elder Cook, Lehi just died." I could see that this woman knew how to hear the voice of the Lord in the scriptures—she was having an experience with the Lord while she was reading. I said, "How many times have you read the Book of Mormon, Sister?" I was quite surprised when she said, "This is my very first time." I was humbled as I saw how the Lord was teaching this woman by the Spirit how to read the scriptures—even as one just beginning to read.

I once had a memorable and spiritual experience with the scriptures in a missionary meeting in Rancagua, Chile. The experience didn't begin as a positive one, however. As the meeting began, we could tell during the opening hymn that the missionaries were really down. They weren't singing energetically. It was as if something had happened that morning to dampen their spirits.

I asked the mission president to have them sing another number with great energy, which they did standing up, and it seemed to help pick up their spirits. The meeting then went forward, and the mission president and his wife spoke. When I

stood to teach, I could tell that they still weren't feeling strong
and positive in spirit.

I began to pray in my heart, and I told them that I didn't
know if I would be able to teach them unless they were really
in tune. But if they would prepare themselves, I would teach
them how to read the scriptures. I told them I would read in
English, so the English-speaking missionaries would have to
translate for their companions. They were to all read the scriptures along with me. The result was a unique experience, one
that has seldom happened in public.

I first read to them from Doctrine and Covenants 35:20 and
25:12, stressing how the Lord felt about things in his own soul
and that the scriptures were from his own bosom. Here are the
scriptures we read:

> And a commandment I give unto thee—that thou
> shalt write for him; and the *scriptures* shall be given, even
> as they *are in mine own bosom,* to the salvation of mine own
> elect. (D&C 35:20; emphasis added.)

> For *my soul delighteth in the song of the heart;* yea, the
> song of the righteous is a prayer unto me, and it shall be
> answered with a blessing upon their heads. (D&C 25:12;
> emphasis added.)

It seemed that as I testified of the Lord, magnifying him
and his greatness, the Spirit swept into the entire room and
almost seemed to lift everyone out of their chairs.

I bore witness of the Lamanites and of Joseph of Egypt and
of the power of the latter-day scriptures, quoting 2 Nephi 3
(looking at verses 6, 9–12, 15, and 19–23). For instance, part of
what we read included these words:

> But a seer will I raise up out of the fruit of thy loins;
> and unto him will I give *power to bring forth my word* unto
> the seed of thy loins—and not to the bringing forth my

word only, saith the Lord, but to the *convincing them of my word,* which shall have already gone forth among them.

Wherefore, the fruit of thy loins shall write; and the fruit of the loins of Judah shall write; and that which shall be written . . . shall grow together, unto the *confounding of false doctrines* and *laying down of contentions,* and *establishing peace* among the fruit of thy loins, and bringing them to the knowledge of their fathers in the latter days, and also to the *knowledge of my covenants,* saith the Lord. . . .

And the words which he shall write shall be the words which are expedient in my wisdom should go forth unto the fruit of thy loins. And it shall be as if the fruit of thy loins had cried unto them from the dust; for I know their faith. And they shall *cry from the dust; yea, even repentance* unto their brethren, even after many generations have gone by them. And it shall come to pass that their cry shall go, even according to the simpleness of their words.

Because of their faith their words shall proceed forth out of my mouth unto their brethren who are the fruit of thy loins; and *the weakness of their words will I make strong in their faith, unto the remembering of my covenant* which I made unto thy fathers. (2 Nephi 3:11–12, 19–21; emphasis added.)

As we read those scriptures, it seemed as if the Lord himself spoke in the meeting. The great love the Lord has for us burned into the heart of every person. We sensed how he considers his scriptures sacred, and how he will speak and testify of the veracity of the scriptures to his servants if they will prepare themselves.

Then we read in 2 Nephi 27:11, where it says,

And the day cometh that the *words of the book* which were sealed shall be *read upon the house tops;* and they shall be *read by the power of Christ;* and all things shall be revealed unto the children of men which ever have been among the children of men, and which ever will be even unto the end of the earth. (Emphasis added.)

And we read that the Lord is going to make his word available to all nations:

Thou shalt ask, and my scriptures shall be given as I have appointed, and they shall be preserved in safety. . . . And I give unto you a commandment that then ye shall teach them unto all men; for they *shall be taught unto all nations, kindreds, tongues and people.* (D&C 42:56, 58; emphasis added.)

As we felt the Spirit in our review of those scriptures, we all greatly rejoiced in what was happening to us in that meeting. I wish I could explain it more fully, but words do not seem to be capable of communicating such a great experience.

I think it is very significant that in the months preceding this meeting I had been praying off and on about how to bring the scriptures alive in the hearts of those who don't seem to have much room for them. Even some Church leaders can sometimes become so involved in other things that they don't seem to have time to immerse themselves in the written words of the Lord.

But I bear testimony to you that there is great power in the words of the Lord. If we will be sure to use them in all the teaching settings we're in, the fruits of the Spirit will begin to come to us and bless those we teach.

INVITE THE SPIRIT THROUGH TESTIMONY

Testify frequently while you are teaching. This is probably as important—and in some cases more so—as *what* you are teaching. Testify in the name of the Lord that the things you are teaching are true. If you will do that, it will bring the Spirit of the Lord.

We ought to make it a regular practice to testify to one another. When things are not going well in your teaching, don't hesitate to stop and say, "I feel impressed to bear my witness to the truthfulness of what I've been saying." And I have found it helpful at times to stop my teaching and ask some in the audience to come up and bear testimony of what they're feeling at that moment. I don't do that to fill up time but because the work of the Lord is carried out by our testimonies. Don't denigrate your own testimony. Bear it powerfully and frequently while you're teaching. Humble testimonies are carried to the hearts of those listening and bring the Spirit of the Lord. As Nephi taught,

> I, Nephi, cannot write all the things which were taught among my people; neither am I mighty in writing, like unto speaking; for when a man speaketh by the power of the Holy Ghost the power of the Holy Ghost carrieth it unto the hearts of the children of men. (2 Nephi 33:1.)

I also hope that we're testifying frequently to our children in our homes. I hope when you're reading in scripture study with your family that you stop and bear your testimony. Invite your children to bear theirs as well. Invite them to testify about a particular principle that you've talked about that very morning.

We should be testifying to the less-active members we home teach or visiting teach. We should do it in interviewing. We should look for other opportunities to bear testimony. Why? Because bearing testimony will bring the Spirit of the Lord, if we do it humbly. We cannot humbly testify of the truth and not have the Spirit immediately come.

The personal testimony of a missionary is an essential part of preparing people to hear the discussions. When we declare with faith the convictions we have about gospel truths, the Holy Ghost will reveal the truth with power to the investigator (see 2 Nephi 33:1–2). He must then use his agency to accept or reject that witness. Our obligation is to declare the truth by the Spirit, to declare testimony in the name of the Lord, to testify from our own life experiences, and then our testimonies will transmit with power.

When Alma saw wickedness increasing among the Nephites, he decided to "go forth among his people, . . . that he might preach the word of God unto them, to stir them up in remembrance of their duty, . . . seeing no way that he might reclaim them save it were in *bearing down in pure testimony* against them" (Alma 4:19; emphasis added).

Later he said:

> I am called to speak after this manner, according to the holy order of God, which is in Christ Jesus; yea, I am commanded to stand and testify unto this people the things which have been spoken by our fathers concerning the things which are to come.
>
> And this is not all. Do ye not suppose that I know of these things myself? Behold, I testify unto you that I do know that these things whereof I have spoken are true. And how do ye suppose that I know of their surety?
>
> Behold, I say unto you they are made known unto me by the Holy Spirit of God. Behold, I have fasted and prayed many days that I might know these things of myself. And now I do know of myself that they are true; for the Lord God hath made them manifest unto me by his Holy Spirit; and this is the spirit of revelation which is in me. (Alma 5:44–46.)

One Saturday when I was serving in Germany, we decided to go swimming at a place with water slides. After swimming a while and sliding a few times, I sat on a little cement ledge near the bottom of one of the slides and watched my children as they came roaring down. After I had been there a few minutes, a lady who was probably about twenty-five or thirty came and sat down next to me. She, too, was watching her children come down the slides. As we sat there I offered a prayer that the Lord would inspire me to know what to say. After a few moments, I said something to her in German about the children sliding and playing in the water. But she didn't seem to understand, and when she finally said, "What?" I knew she spoke English.

With my limited understanding of German, that was even better. We started to visit. I learned that she and her husband were with the U.S. military in Germany. She asked who I was and what I did. I told her I was with the LDS Church and was in Germany supervising the missionaries in Europe. To my surprise, later in the conversation she finally told me that she was an inactive member of the Church, and her husband was a non-member.

We visited for a while, and as we did I utilized some of the approaches mentioned in this book—I tried to keep a prayer in my heart; I quoted scripture to her; and I issued a challenge, telling her that she needed to find a way to her husband's heart, and that she needed to put her own life in order and come back into activity so they could be sealed in the house of the Lord. I told her that I knew the Lord would bless her, and bore a strong testimony of the truthfulness of the things I'd been saying. By then my children were ready to go and I told her good-bye and left.

A couple of months later I received a phone call from two missionaries. They said, "Elder Cook, we understand you went swimming with this married lady." I said, "Wait a minute—what married lady?" Then they reminded me about this lady I had met at the pool. They told me that after we talked she began to feel the spirit of what I had said to her, and she told her husband that very day that she had met a General Authority of the Church. She repeated what we'd talked about and bore her testimony to him. A couple of days later, she and her husband were visiting a big shopping mall in Frankfurt, and these missionaries approached them seemingly out of the blue. Can you imagine the probability of that with the thousands of people in the mall? The husband's heart was softened, and he agreed to let the missionaries teach them in their home. During the third or fourth lesson, if I remember correctly, she identified me in a picture of all the General Authorities. In a matter of a few weeks more, the wife was reactivated and the husband had joined the Church.

I don't know what I said to her that made the difference—and the truth is that *I* didn't make the difference. But somehow the Lord spoke through a weak instrument and conveyed a word that brought about some humility on her part. Because someone was willing to open his mouth and bear testimony, the Spirit was able to come into her heart and begin to bless her.

There is great power in bearing your testimony. Remember, "when a man speaketh by the power of the Holy Ghost the power of the Holy Ghost carrieth it unto the hearts of the children of men" (2 Nephi 33:1). I bear testimony that that is exactly what happens.

INVITE THE SPIRIT BY USING THE HYMNS

If you want to invite the Spirit into a teaching experience, sing a hymn. Throughout the history of the Church, singing hymns has been an important preparation to worship. Hymns are prayers of faith and righteousness. Blessings from heaven come as a result of singing sacred hymns.

Music has a great impact on the souls of men. For many years now, we have had a practice in our home of singing when we have family prayer—both in the mornings and in the evenings. I am not suggesting this as something every family must do, but we have found it very helpful when we all kneel down in a circle to sing a hymn before we pray. Such singing calms and quiets little ones who may be "punching their neighbor" or fidgeting. It prepares our hearts so that we begin to think of the Lord; we begin to feel the Spirit—and then we pray.

I never really knew many of the Primary songs because I didn't have the opportunity to go to Primary much when I was younger. But my children and my good wife have taught me many wonderful Primary songs as we have sung together before our family prayers.

The hymns of the Church will bring the Spirit of the Lord into a setting immediately. It would certainly not be inappropriate, if need be, to stop in the middle of your teaching and say, "Let's sing a hymn together," and then pick a hymn that relates to what you are teaching. I've known some priesthood leaders that have sung in an interview with a sister or brother. "What do you think, we're not doing too well in this interview, why don't we sing a song together?" That takes a little boldness, but it works. If you are ever personally down a little bit, get in the habit of singing to yourself. Sing those sacred hymns, and they will fill you with the Spirit of the Lord.

We learn of this blessing from the Old Testament:

> And it came to pass, when the evil spirit, which was not of God, was upon Saul, that David took a harp, and played with his hand; so Saul was refreshed, and was well, and the evil spirit departed from him. (JST, 1 Samuel 16:23.)

Some time ago I was with a member of the Quorum of the Twelve at an area training meeting for some stake presidents. At one point in one of the meetings, when the Spirit seemed to be waning a little, the member of the Twelve stopped the meeting and said, "Let's stop right here and sing 'Does the Journey Seem Long?'" We did so. It "just so happened" that that hymn seemed to be just what those brethren needed at that moment, and from then on the influence of the Spirit in the meeting significantly increased.

When I was serving in Germany, I was impressed with an experience two missionaries had in Hamburg. We'd been teaching the missionaries to sing to the people. These two elders were trying to speak to a lady on her doorstep, and she was turning them away. They said, "But we have prepared a song to sing to you." She said, "What, you mean right here on my porch?" And the elders answered, "Yes, we could. But it would be better inside. We're ready to sing." She said, "Okay, come in."

They sang to her. When they were finished, she wrote out a thousand mark check (that's about $600) and said, "Two young men who can sing like that need this money." These elders weren't sure if that was a compliment or not, but they did know that the woman had felt the Spirit.

But they said to her, "We can't take your money."

"Oh, no, this is for you."

"No, we can't take your money. What we want to do is teach you." So she opened her home to them and let them teach her a gospel lesson. A couple of weeks later the mission president received a thousand mark check from this woman, inviting him to use it for missionary purposes, which he did. Even more important, by the time I heard this story while touring the mission, the lady had already received the third missionary discussion.

This story shows again the power of gospel hymns. This woman, a nonmember of the Church, was so touched that she allowed the missionaries to teach her a lesson and then made a $600 donation to the Church.

In another experience in this same mission, the missionaries found a Russian man who could not speak a word of German, and they could not speak a word of Russian. But they were able to communicate to him that they would like him to come to church on Sunday. He visited their ward three Sundays in a row, not understanding a single word. Finally they found somebody who could interpret for them. When they finally sat down to teach him, the first thing he said to them was, "Who wrote those hymns in your church?"

They said, "What do you mean?"

And he said, "They are of the Lord." He didn't understand a single word of the hymns. But he felt the power of the songs, and he felt how they helped him to feel the Spirit of the Lord.

Paul admonished us:

> Let the word of Christ dwell in you richly in all wisdom; teaching and admonishing one another in psalms and hymns and spiritual songs, singing with grace in your hearts to the Lord. (Colossians 3:16.)

Remember, music is a valuable way to touch people's hearts and bring them back to Christ.

The great spiritual influence of music was described by the Lord in a very personal statement about Himself. There are not very many passages where he speaks *personally*, but in Doctrine and Covenants 25:12 he says:

> For my soul [here he talks of his very own soul!] *delighteth* in the song of the heart; yea, the song of the righteous is a prayer unto me, and it shall be answered with a blessing upon their heads. (Emphasis added.)

I desire such a blessing upon my head, as do you. There is great power in sacred hymns. They are not just songs; they are prayers to God. Sing them that way and they will help you humble yourself, and they will help to bring the Spirit into your teaching.

INVITE THE SPIRIT BY EXPRESSING LOVE AND GRATITUDE TO GOD AND MAN

It is impossible to humbly express your love for the Lord, sharing how you really feel in your heart about him, and to express your love for one another, and not have the Spirit of the Lord come upon you.

At the same time, you cannot humbly express your love to someone else and not have a response from that individual. And you cannot humbly express your love to the Lord in front of other people and not have a spiritual response from them.

Love has tremendous power. No wonder the scriptures say that "God is love" (1 John 4:8, 16). At the end of our family prayers, we throw our arms around each of our children, grab them tight, and whisper, "I love you." Sometimes unkind words and tense feelings can be melted away in a simple embrace; that can sometimes go further than anything you could say. Be sure to express your love amply to your students, to your children, and to the Lord, and the Spirit will be with you in that very instant. Love will bring the Spirit *right now* if it finds a humble heart.

The same is true of gratitude, of counting our blessings. I wonder if we count our blessings enough. When we express gratitude to the Lord for all he has given us, when we express gratitude to others for what they do for us, we begin to feel more humble. It can't be just an expression of words, of course. We have to express what is truly in our hearts. Then, if we are really feeling that love and gratitude, they will feel it as well. And the Spirit will come.

The scriptures teach us of the need for pure love—and the great blessing it brings into our lives:

> And the angel said unto me: Behold the Lamb of God, yea, even the Son of the Eternal Father! Knowest thou the meaning of the tree which thy father saw?
>
> And I answered him, saying: Yea, it is the love of God, which sheddeth itself abroad in the hearts of the children of men; wherefore, it is the most desirable above all things.

And he spake unto me, saying: Yea, and the most joyous to the soul. (1 Nephi 11:21–23.)

But charity is the pure love of Christ, and it endureth forever; and whoso is found possessed of it at the last day, it shall be well with him.

Wherefore, my beloved brethren, pray unto the Father with all the energy of heart, that ye may be filled with this love, which he hath bestowed upon all who are true followers of his Son, Jesus Christ; that ye may become the sons of God; that when he shall appear we shall be like him, for we shall see him as he is; that we may have this hope; that we may be purified even as he is pure. (Moroni 7:47–48.)

A new commandment I give unto you, That ye love one another; as I have loved you, that ye also love one another. By this shall all men know that ye are my disciples, if ye have love one to another. (John 13:34–35.)

Some time ago I was in Rome and was having a problem with my airline ticket home. One of the missionaries accompanied me as I went into the airport to clear it up. The young woman working at the Alitalia counter, who was about twenty-five or so, was very gracious and very helpful. She went the extra mile to help me, making a special effort to get me onto a plane to Frankfurt, Germany, where my family was living at the time. After she finished I called her by name (I could read her name tag; I'll call her Maria) and said, "I want you to know how grateful I am for what you have done. I wanted to be home with my family tonight. They mean the world to me, and they will be very happy to have their dad come home. Thanks so much; you have gone out of your way to make sure that a customer was pleased. You have a wonderful spirit about you. You are a credit to Alitalia. I want you to know I greatly appreciate your effort. Thank you for your goodness to me."

Maria was unable to speak for a moment, and I could tell

she was moved. The tears flowed. Finally she said, "That's about the nicest thing anybody's ever said to me."

Then I said, because I knew we were all feeling the Spirit, "Do you know who this young man is right here?" And I pointed to the missionary.

She said, "I have no idea." She couldn't read his name tag because he was standing back a little. She strained to read it and said aloud (in Italian), "The Church of Jesus Christ of Latter-day Saints."

"I don't like my own church," she said, and she named it and told us of an experience she had had in her church that had really soured her. She then said, "Would it be possible for someone like me to attend one of your meetings?" We told her we thought we could arrange that and took her name and telephone number. The last I heard she did indeed attend our Church and was being taught by the missionaries.

Just after I returned from my mission, my bishop called me to be the assistant clerk in our ward. As I found myself in different settings in the ward, occasionally members would discuss a Sister Smith who lived in our ward. I heard comments like, "Well, you know how Sister Smith is," or "Home teaching Sister Smith is no picnic; in fact, home teachers haven't been in her home for the past two years," or "Sister Smith is the worst housekeeper in the ward," or "Sister Smith does nothing but mope around her house and collect newspapers. If you went to her home you would see newspapers on her porch and stacked to the ceiling in her living room." I thought, "I hope I never get assigned as a home teacher to Sister Smith."

One day my younger brother and I were in a market purchasing some groceries for my mother. As we walked out, the thought came to me, "Why don't you go back behind this store and see Sister Smith?" I was a little surprised at the thought, and probably from curiosity more than anything else, I said to my brother, "Why don't we go back and see where Sister Smith lives?" I suppose the idea was, "We'll see if everything people have said about her house is true."

As we went around the back of the store and looked at her home from a distance, we could see that at least some of the stories were true. The house was dilapidated. The fence was broken down and unpainted, and her yard was full of junk. As we stood there, an impression came: "Go visit Sister Smith." I was taken aback and thought, "I'm not her home teacher." But the impression continued: "Go visit Sister Smith."

I said to my brother, "Let's go visit her." He was surprised, but nonetheless we headed for the door. I remember praying rather intently, "What shall I say? What will we do? Why are we going there?" As we entered her yard, we saw the newspapers. Sure enough, they were stacked all over the porch. I could see through the window that newspapers were stacked inside her house as well.

We knocked on the door. She opened it and rather gruffly said, "What is it? What do you want?" I struggled to know what to say, but finally I blurted out, "Well, we're members of your ward." The moment the word ward came out, she said, "You mean you're Mormons? I've told that bishop ten times not to send anybody to my home. I want nothing to do with the Mormon church, so leave." As I prayed in my heart what to say, the words came out, "Well, Sister Smith, this is my younger brother, and he and I just came by to tell you that we love you. Even if you don't particularly care about us, we do love you. We just wanted to ask if there was anything we could do to help you today."

She stood there staring at us and finally said, "What did you say?"

I repeated myself, trying to have her really feel of our love.

She said, "You've come to ask if you could help me?" Then tears came to her eyes. Then lots of tears. She invited us in. We spent nearly two hours listening as she told us about her problems.

She apologized for the condition of her house and yard. She told us about the leak in her roof. She said she had no one to help her—she didn't have any family. She told us about her problems at the death of her husband a few years earlier when she had felt offended by some Church members. She just poured out her tears. She got it all out. We rejoiced, perhaps more than she did, in finally seeing all the bitterness come forth.

You can imagine the joy my brother and I felt as we accompanied her to church the next Sunday, and she attended church many other Sundays until she passed away about six months later.

I've often thought, "What if we had not responded to the promptings? What if we had not been told what to say?" It surely would not have turned out the same way.

As I have reflected on those experiences, I have wondered why Maria and Sister Smith were so responsive. Sometimes it's hard to get people to listen to the missionaries or home teachers; why were these sisters so willing? The answer is that they felt the love of the Lord through a simple expression of love and gratitude. I think when someone truly feels the love of God, they humble themselves, they're responsive, and the Spirit comes to bless them.

INVITE THE SPIRIT BY SHARING SPIRITUAL EXPERIENCES

Share a spiritual experience if you want to increase the Spirit in a setting. When the Lord was teaching, he didn't just quote Isaiah and other scripture to the disciples, though that was an essential part of his teaching. But he also told many stories. A real teacher by the Spirit will learn to do the same thing. He will pull from his own life and the lives of others spiritual experiences that illustrate a principle and bring the Spirit into the teaching. It is easier for us to apply a truth if we can see it in action in someone else's life. And it is easier to commit to live a truth if we can feel the Spirit through those experiences of other people.

Some people have said to me, "Well, Elder Cook, it's easy for you to tell stories. You have so many great experiences. But I don't even know one single story from my own life." To them I say, "Well, maybe you don't, but the Lord does. You've had a lot of spiritual experiences, but you may not have recognized them. The Lord can pull them out of you if you believe that he will, if you will pray for the blessing, and if you practice doing it. Sometimes you can take the simplest experience that happened only an hour before and teach a powerful lesson from it—if you're being observant. Learn to observe all the 'little things' going on around you, and you will find you have many more experiences and stories to tell."

I also believe it is more effective if we don't tell the same stories all the time. Don't just have some repertoire of experiences you traditionally tell (although it's good to have a repertoire), but constantly pray that the Lord will draw from you the one experience that you really ought to share today. If the Lord prompts you to tell a story, you'll be more likely to feel an increase of the Spirit in your teaching.

Paul gave us a great model of a spiritual experience when he said to King Agrippa:

> My manner of life from my youth, . . . know all the Jews; . . . after the most straitest sect of our religion I lived a Pharisee. . . .
>
> I verily thought with myself, that I ought to do many things contrary to the name of Jesus of Nazareth. Which thing I also did in Jerusalem: and many of the saints did I shut up in prison, having received authority from the chief priests; and when they were put to death, I gave my voice against them. And I punished them oft in every synagogue, and . . . I persecuted them even unto strange cities.

Whereupon as I went to Damascus with authority and commission from the chief priests, at midday, O king, I saw in the way a light from heaven, above the brightness of the sun, shining round about me and them which journeyed with me. And when we were all fallen to the earth, I heard a voice speaking unto me, and saying in the Hebrew tongue, Saul, Saul, why persecutest thou me? it is hard for thee to kick against the pricks.

And I said, Who art thou, Lord? And he said, I am Jesus whom thou persecutest. But rise, and stand upon thy feet: for I have appeared unto thee for this purpose, to make thee a minister and a witness both of these things which thou hast seen, and of those things in the which I will appear unto thee. . . .

Whereupon, O king Agrippa, I was not disobedient unto the heavenly vision: But shewed first unto them of Damascus, and at Jerusalem, and throughout all the coasts of Judaea, and then to the Gentiles, that they should repent and turn to God, and do works meet for repentance. For these causes the Jews caught me in the temple, and went about to kill me.

Having therefore obtained help of God, I continue unto this day, witnessing both to small and great, saying none other things than those which the prophets and Moses did say should come: That Christ should suffer, and that he should be the first that should rise from the dead, and should shew light unto the people, and to the Gentiles. . . .

Then Agrippa said unto Paul, Almost thou persuadest me to be a Christian. (Acts 26:4–5, 9–16, 19–23, 28.)

We must be cautious with spiritual experiences, however. There is a time for sharing these experiences and a time not to do so. There are some experiences that ought to be shared and some that ought not be shared. Alma gave us this counsel:

It is given unto many to know the mysteries of God; nevertheless they are laid under a strict command that they shall not impart only according to the portion of his word which he doth grant unto the children of men, according to the heed and diligence which they give unto him.

And therefore, he that will harden his heart, the same receiveth the lesser portion of the word; and he that will not harden his heart, to him is given the greater portion of the word, until it is given unto him to know the mysteries of God until he know them in full. (Alma 12:9–10.)

If you're sensitive to the Spirit, you will find that the Lord will tell you what to share and when, and that may be at the very moment when your experience will totally turn someone else around. Or the Spirit may direct you not to share something that is particularly personal or deeply spiritual, because it may have been given only for you or because others may misunderstand or treat lightly the sacred experience you share.

Think of how the experiences shared in this book have enlivened the text. I believe they have made a great difference in conveying the teachings and the doctrine we've discussed. The same is true in any teaching situation—the lessons will be learned better and felt deeper if you share genuine examples and spiritual experiences.

Remember, the number one objective of a teacher is to help *create an environment where the student can have a spiritual experience.* And one way to do that is to share, as appropriate, your own spiritual experiences or those from Church history or other sources.

INVITE THE SPIRIT THROUGH PRIESTHOOD BLESSINGS

Finally, we can invite the Spirit by giving a priesthood blessing. Such a blessing will greatly enhance and bring the Spirit of the Lord into a setting. In our families blessings ought to be given quite frequently: when a family member is having a particular challenge or where you just have a fine and faithful son or daughter and you wish to allow the Lord to commend them through a loving priesthood blessing.

We can also sometimes be directed by the Spirit to use priesthood blessings in our other stewardships.

While I was visiting and teaching the missionaries in Dresden, Germany, some time ago, the mission president asked me to visit with an elder who was determined to go home early. The mission president had worked with the missionary for several months, but had not succeeded in changing his mind.

During our interview, I found the young man to be a worthy elder who had really desired to go on a mission. I was amazed that he wanted to go home early. But as we visited it seemed evident that he was being influenced by the evil one. I asked him to describe the fruits of the Spirit he had felt as he saw people being taught the gospel. Then I asked him to describe the influence of the evil one. He spoke of the feelings he had suffered with for the previous few months—darkness, discouragement, confusion, anger, and so forth.

When I bore testimony to him that I believed he was being influenced by the devil, he remembered similar struggles he had had in the past. I suggested a priesthood blessing, and he was very desirous to receive one. His mission president and I then blessed him. Through the Spirit, he was promised protection and safety from the evil influence so he could obtain what he needed spiritually in order to be a great missionary.

In reports I received later, the mission president bore testimony that on that very day, during the priesthood blessing, the evil influence had been cast away from this elder. From that time forward he became a wonderful missionary and served valiantly in the mission.

I had been very impressed with this young man's spirit. He had apparently been brought up in an inactive family, and his entire future could have been very different if on that particular day the Lord had not intervened. He may have returned home from his mission early and joined his family in inactivity. But the Lord, through his grace and mercy, ministered to this elder, touched his heart, and turned him into a great instrument in the mission field. When he returned home, he surely was a positive influence on his family and many others as a result of the Lord's blessing in turning his life around.

Through that priesthood blessing that day, the mission president and I were able to obtain a gift of the presence of the Spirit in our counseling with that young elder. We had tried to teach him true and important principles about staying on his mission and continuing in faithful service, but it was only through the priesthood blessing that he was able to truly receive what he needed most.

I believe that priesthood blessings are a gift the Lord would like to give us much more often than we allow him to. Perhaps we don't want to bother anyone for a blessing, or maybe we aren't humble enough. Maybe we think: "I can handle this. I don't need the Lord's help with this problem. I can handle it." But the truth is that the Lord invites us to utilize the priesthood he has given to the Church, to receive the blessings he offers, to grow in the Spirit through this means.

Of course, blessings are primarily to be given in the home or, as appropriate, in the bishop's office. If a student came to ask me for a blessing, I would probably do my best to steer him home to his father. I would say, "Your dad's a member, isn't he?" "Well, yeah, but he's inactive." "Well, let me give you a few suggestions about what you could do to get your dad to give you a blessing." And that could lead to some great instruction.

President Benson tells a story of a man who came to him pleading for a priesthood blessing. This was an adult man who had never had a blessing because his father had been inactive all his life. President Benson took the time to teach that man how to obtain a blessing from his father. The man did go and ask his inactive dad to give him a blessing and that sweet experience helped reactivate the whole family. Thus, I would turn a student first to his or her father.

If that were not appropriate, then I would try to steer them to their home teacher, the bishop, or a priesthood leader. If they really persist because of some special relationship with you, I would recommend you call the family or the bishop to clear it, saying that so-and-so has asked for a blessing and you'd like to do that if it is all right with them. Of course, in an emergency situation or if you felt inspired on the spot, you might feel to provide such a blessing in the very moment.

Doctrine and Covenants 24:13–14 says, in part,

> Require not miracles, except . . . healing the sick, . . . and these things ye shall not do, except it be required of you by them who desire it.

Some have misinterpreted this to mean that we should never volunteer to give another person a blessing. That's only partly true. Let me explain what I mean.

A few years ago I was serving in Central America when a serious earthquake occurred. Some ten thousand people were killed, including several members of the Church. Many homes were destroyed. That first evening I went into an LDS meeting-house where we were housing some of the injured. It was dark in the building, since the electricity was out. People were suffering, and they didn't have any medicine. The first three people I came to had difficult injuries. I said, "Have you had a priesthood blessing?" Each person said "No." I was quite surprised. I went out in the hall with a bishop who was accompanying me and said, "Bishop, why haven't these folks had blessings?" He said, "No one has asked me, Elder Cook. I couldn't give a blessing unless I was asked, could I?"

What do we do when someone obviously needs a blessing but doesn't ask?

I would recommend we review with them the counsel in James 5:14–16, which says,

> Is any sick among you? let him call for the elders of the church; and let them pray over him, anointing him with oil in the name of the Lord: and the prayer of faith shall save the sick, and the Lord shall raise him up; and if he have committed sins, they shall be forgiven him.
>
> Confess your faults one to another, and pray one for another, that ye may be healed. The effectual fervent prayer of a righteous man availeth much.

You might say to a less-active man, for example, "Brother Brown, I wonder if you would like to have a blessing. You may have forgotten what that's all about, but as you will remember, the Lord taught us that when there are sick, we are to lay hands upon them, and if faith is present, the Lord will heal them. I bear witness to you of the great power of the priesthood," and then maybe bear testimony to them with the Spirit of the Lord.

It's a fine line we walk here. The Lord wants people to ask for a blessing because it's a measure of their faith. But many people are either not sensitive enough to ask or they have forgotten and they need that gentle spiritual reminder. We can at least set the stage and then, hopefully, they'll say to us, "Would you mind giving me a blessing?"

The best scenario, of course, is when the person receiving the blessing is filled with faith and desire. I think of the woman whose faith was so strong that she "came behind him, and touched the hem of his garment: For she said within herself, If I may but touch his garment, I shall be whole" (Matthew 9:20–21). After she touched the hem of his robe she was healed instantly. Then Jesus turned and asked who had touched him as he perceived that virtue, or power, had left him. When the woman revealed herself, Jesus said, "Daughter, be of good comfort; thy faith hath made thee whole" (Matthew 9:22; see also Mark 5:34).

There is great power in the faith of the one who is going to receive a blessing. They must make an offering of a pure heart and a contrite spirit, and if they will pay that price, they will see the Spirit of the Lord respond to them through a healing, if that is the will of the Lord.

I've made it a practice when I've been about to give someone a blessing to invite that person to kneel down with me and my companion and offer a prayer first. This is probably more for their benefit than anything else, to make sure their heart was humbled before the blessing was given. I like the scripture that says, "After they had prayed unto the Father in the name of Christ, they laid their hands upon them." (Moroni 3:2; see also D&C 42:44). I have also found it very beneficial before a blessing to read a few passages about healings or to bear my testimony to them.

There is another kind of blessing that also brings the Spirit into a teaching situation. The scriptures tell us that when we go into a home we ought to leave a blessing on that home (see D&C 75:18–19; Luke 10:5–9). This is commonly done by missionaries and home teachers. It can surely be done to help bless individuals and families (both member and nonmember, both those who are active and less active) as we seek to teach by the Spirit in their homes.

As directed by the Spirit, at the appropriate moment simply turn to the head of the household and ask "May we, as servants of the Lord, leave a blessing on you and your home?" When he says yes, kneel and invite them to join you. Offer a sincere prayer and invoke the blessings of heaven upon the father, the mother, and the children, mentioning each one by name, if possible. If you hold the priesthood, do it by the power of the priesthood. If you are a sister, you can still kneel and, through the prayer of faith, ask the Lord to invoke his blessings upon the family. Following the prayer, you will often sense a different spirit and can then invite the father and the family to listen to the message you bring. If they do not want to listen, leave graciously and know you have left a blessing upon that home.

Certainly this suggestion is difficult to apply in the classroom, because that isn't an appropriate setting for these kinds of blessings. But when you are visiting people in their homes or when you are in your own home, priesthood blessings can be powerful. Such blessings surely bring the Spirit.

A TRIANGLE OF SPIRITUAL INFLUENCE AND LOVE

How does the Spirit come into a setting and change the hearts of the people involved? What does the teacher with the Spirit (a parent, missionary, leader, home teacher) do to assist the learner (a child, an investigator, a less-active family, a spouse) who may not be feeling the Spirit?

First of all (using the example of a father and a teenage son), the *parent must turn to the Lord.*

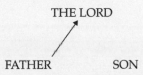

When the parent humbly and prayerfully seeks the help of the Lord, *the Lord will send his Spirit.*

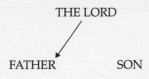

Next, in a spirit of love and with the help of the Holy Ghost, *the father will turn to his son, teaching him what is needed.*

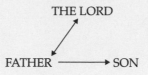

Third, *the son, in humility, turns himself to the Lord.*

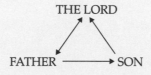

In response, *the Lord sends his Spirit to the son.*

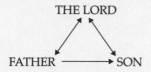

The triangle becomes complete when *the son, in humility, turns back to the father,* willing to do what he was taught.

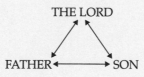

This triangle of influence and love demonstrates a way to teach any important truth. When a teacher uses this approach, and when the student responds in the Spirit, humility and true learning is the inevitable result. The son will turn to the father and say, "Dad, what shall I do? Tell me what to do, and I will do it." Or the nonmember will say to the missionary, "I'll do anything you tell me. What shall I do?" Or the member in the

Gospel Doctrine class will turn to the teacher and say, "I believe all you have said. What shall I do now?"

Such a response comes when the teacher turns to the Lord and receives his Spirit; then the teacher turns the student, not to himself, but to the Lord. The mortal teacher can communicate information, but only the Spirit of the Lord can touch, soften, and change the hearts of people.

This triangle reinforces another truth: that the best thing we can do in teaching is to help the listener have an experience with the Spirit of the Lord. If we have accomplished that, we will have helped to open a door to real learning.

COUNSEL AND A CAUTION

I would recommend that whenever you teach, you try to incorporate some or all of the seven principles discussed in this chapter, or others you may know. They will invite the Spirit to be present so that when truths are taught, they will be received by the hearts of the people. These principles will greatly aid you in teaching by the Spirit.

But these principles work only on one condition: We must humble ourselves. You can sing a hymn without being humble and you won't get a thing out of it. You can pray without being humble and you won't get anything out of it.

The same is true of the person being taught: He or she also must be humble, or the process won't work. In fact, the whole purpose of these suggestions is to prepare an environment that will help the "student" to humble himself before the Lord. He must come to a repentant spirit. He must be lowly in heart before he will *receive* the word of the Lord from the Lord's servants.

After the "student" has felt the Spirit and has humbled himself in his heart, he will be repentant and will ask the key question we all must ask: "What shall we do?" This will then allow the mortal teacher, as well as the Spirit of God, to more fully teach him the things the Lord would have him know.

I challenge each of us to work at teaching by the Spirit more effectively. Ask every time you're called on to give a talk, teach a lesson, conduct a leadership meeting, or conduct an interview: "Could this be done more by the Spirit? Am I willing to risk a little more to see if the Lord will speak through me?"

I know from experience that sometimes things don't come out very polished. You may stumble; you may repeat yourself two or three times. Don't worry about that, and don't judge yourself. The Lord has many ways of working through us, and sometimes he may do so in what you might consider a rather awkward or unpolished way. That in itself may more fully humble you—and that's okay too.

One caution: Be careful of trying to put the Spirit into some pattern or list of things that seemingly will help you dictate to or control the Spirit. The Lord offers certain blessings when we obey certain principles, but we are to *ask for* and to *invite* the Spirit, not try to put it all in our control. The Spirit will be a great aid to us, but we must not feel as if it is totally under our direction. I believe with all my heart that there are certain things we can do to set up the environment so that the Spirit will come. But sometimes that blessing doesn't come as we expected. Perhaps the reason is that the faith of those in the room is lacking, or they are impure and unworthy, or maybe the Lord has reasons of his own that we do not understand.

Let us not seek to dictate to the Lord or his Spirit. But at the same time, let us diligently seek, according to true principles, to receive all the blessings of the Lord by faithfully *inviting* his Spirit to be with us in all we do. That counsel is clearly understood in these words:

> Yea, . . . cry unto God for all thy support; yea, let all
> thy doings be unto the Lord, and whithersoever thou
> goest let it be in the Lord; yea, let all thy thoughts be

directed unto the Lord; yea, let the affections of thy heart be placed upon the Lord forever.

Counsel with the Lord in all thy doings, and he will direct thee for good; yea, when thou liest down at night lie down unto the Lord, that he may watch over you in your sleep; and when thou risest in the morning let thy heart be full of thanks unto God; and if ye do these things, ye shall be lifted up at the last day. (Alma 37:36–37.)

As I said before, the single greatest thing a teacher can do is provide the environment so that the people can have a spiritual experience. And how does the teacher do that? These seven spiritual principles will help you to provide such an experience. I pray we may all humbly learn how to do it better, that the hearts of the people may truly be humbled and turned to the Lord.

QUESTIONS TO PONDER

1. What changes can you make in your family to invite a greater abundance of the Spirit into your home?

_____

_____

_____

2. What might you do when you are teaching and you can't feel the Spirit?

_____

_____

_____

3. What might you do when you are teaching and the class or individual to whom you are speaking is not feeling the Spirit?

_____

_____

_____

4. How do you handle the fears of the natural man that might prevent you from "taking the risk" to speak more as you are inspired "in the very moment"?

_____

_____

_____

5. How could you improve on the spirituality of your visits as a visiting teacher or home teacher?

_____

_____

_____

CHAPTER 6

THE ROLE
OF THE LEARNER

Good teaching isn't just the responsibility of the teacher. For real learning to take place, the learner also has a great responsibility. Remember: "He that is . . . sent forth to preach the word of truth [must] preach it by the Spirit" or "it is not of God." Also, "he that receiveth the word of truth [must] receive it by the Spirit" or "it is not of God" (D&C 50:17–20).

I would like to share an example of a man who acted diligently in the role of a learner to his great blessing. In 1983 I met a Protestant minister when I spoke at a Latter-day Saint meeting in California to which nonmembers of the Church had been invited. Mr. Jones (I have not used his real name) was touched by what he felt in that San Diego meeting and somewhat taken aback by the fact that "even Mormons have the Spirit." I was impressed with him when we first met; I felt a great spirit in him.

He had congregations in California and in several places in Latin America where he preached, but he accepted my invitation to take time to attend our general conference in October 1983. He seemed deeply touched by the fulness of the doctrine of Jesus Christ that he heard in the conference sessions. Over the next four years, we had a number of encounters on the telephone and in person. His married daughter and her husband received the gospel and joined the Church in Germany. I challenged him to receive the missionary lessons also, and he did. He became converted to many of the truths he found in the Book of Mormon and taught them to his congregations without disclosing their source.

Then, after four years of Mr. Jones's struggle to obtain sufficient testimony and faith to be baptized, something happened that changed his life. It followed a telephone conversation in which I told him, basically, that the Lord would not wait on him much longer. He had been given a number of witnesses that the Book of Mormon was true, and he needed to act on this knowledge. I challenged him to seek a final confirmation and then to be baptized. He told me how serious this decision was for him—if he were baptized, he would lose his employment, his car, his retirement fund, and so forth. He said, "I have to know for certain."

In the course of our conversation, I asked him to explain to me once again how he was reading the Book of Mormon. He said he was reading it to find out *if it were true.* While we were talking, it dawned on him that he had never read the Bible that way; he had always read it in faith that it was from the Lord, and then he had sought confirmation of its truths. He had a change of spiritual perspective as he realized that the process for reading the Book of Mormon should be exactly the same. He promised me that he would honestly ask God in the same manner; he would treat the Book of Mormon as truth—as the word of God, like the Bible—and would humbly and receptively seek a confirmation.

A day or so later, Brother Jones called to tell me that he had had a tremendous spiritual experience in which the truthfulness of the Book of Mormon was confirmed to him, and he was now ready to be baptized. He said that after confirmation of the truth had come to him by the Spirit, he had received added assurance through a familiar means—inspiration to turn to specific scriptural references.

This had happened to him before. In times past when he had been studying the Bible or preaching, he had found that a particular biblical reference—such as Isaiah 6:7—might suddenly come into his mind. When he looked up the scripture, he would find that it dealt with the very topic or problem at hand. Because this had worked for him so frequently, he determined to try the same test with latter-day scriptures.

He prayed, "Father, if this book is true—and I'm feeling these feelings confirming that it is—then help me know that it is, talking with me through the scriptures the way thou hast done in the Bible." Immediately flashed into his mind Doctrine and Covenants 17:3. He looked up the scripture: "And after that you have obtained faith, and have seen them [the Book of Mormon plates or, in his instance, the printed Book of Mormon] with your eyes, you shall testify of them, by the power of God."

Deeply moved by that response, he nevertheless asked, "Lord, wouldst thou do it one more time, as thou hast said that 'in the mouth of two or three witnesses shall every word be established' [2 Corinthians 13:1]?" Immediately Alma 13:6 came to his mind: "And thus being called by this holy calling, and ordained unto the high priesthood of the holy order of God, to teach his commandments unto the children of men, that they also might enter into his rest." He then felt a strong witness that the Lord was calling him to a holy calling in the true Church and that he would be ordained to the high priesthood in order to teach the Lord's commandments to the children of men.

Then he prayed again humbly, as did Gideon, "Let not thine anger be hot against me" (Judges 6:39), and he asked the Lord to give him just one more witness that he was truly deciding correctly. As he prayed, a reference came into his mind—Moroni 6:3: "And none were received unto baptism save they took upon them the name of Christ, having a determination to serve him to the end." That verse and the verses immediately surrounding it pressed heavily upon him and convinced him that he must be baptized and be "cleansed by the power of the Holy Ghost" (v. 4).

I had the privilege of baptizing him, his wife, and all of his children but one. A number of members of his old church were also baptized. A year later, I had the privilege of sealing him and his wife and children in the Los Angeles Temple.

Brother Jones's experience taught me again how generous our Father in Heaven is in giving us the opportunity to find truth through the spiritual process prescribed in the scriptures. Brother Jones sought diligently to know the truth. He searched and prayed and sought to obey what he was learning. But he wasn't certain about what he should do until he truly opened his heart and listened to the Spirit, receiving the things the Lord wanted to testify to him.

The principles taught in this story are powerful, and they can be employed by all people who seek to learn and grow in the gospel. In this chapter we will talk about a variety of principles of learning, each of which can help us to exercise our agency to draw closer to the Spirit and learn the things the Lord would have us know.

Learning in a Meeting

Someone once asked President Spencer W. Kimball, "What do you do if you find yourself caught in a boring sacrament meeting?" President Kimball thought a moment, then replied, "I don't know; I've never been in one."

What was President Kimball really saying about sacrament meetings? Did he mean that every meeting he had ever attended had featured skillful, well-prepared speakers? Had he never heard a speaker present his material in a dry, dull way, or digress from the topic of his talk? President Kimball's reply indicates a key principle to effective worship: he was saying that the meeting was between him and the Lord; the exact content of the meeting—the talks, prayers, and so on—was somewhat incidental.

Every time we attend a Church meeting, we need to keep focused on the fact that we are there to worship the Lord, to bring souls to the Lord. That focus on the Lord, I believe, is what brings the Spirit in greater abundance into our meetings, not only helping us to worship meaningfully but benefiting all present at the meeting and therefore actually *improving the quality of the meeting.* Yes, our worship has something to do with the speaker up front. It has something to do with the music, because we're worshipping the Lord through the music. But mostly it has to do with our individual ability to worship the Lord in the meeting. I pray that we will have that kind of focus and that we will teach others to also focus on the Lord, so that there will be great power in our Church meetings.

Think of it this way: You're not just attending a meeting between you and the speaker; you're trying to attend a meeting that includes you, the speaker, and the Lord. If you can get into *that* meeting, you will feel the Spirit touch you. You will hear the voice of the Lord speaking truths to you in that very meeting, truths that will move you and touch you in specific ways, triggering thoughts about things you need to be doing differently. Hopefully you'll leave that meeting a better person.

President Marion G. Romney taught that there are three important levels of teaching, in order of priority:

1. What *commitments did you make* as a result of the teaching?

2. What *did you feel* as a result of the teaching?

3. What *did you learn* as a result of the teaching?

When we ask each other, "What did you learn in the meeting?" we need to remember that what we *learned* is the third-place priority. More important is what we *felt* or what we *committed to do* as a result of the meeting. Perhaps that is the highest level of inspired teaching.

PRAYING THROUGH THE MEETING

There are times when a speaker who has given a fine address in a meeting could say, as was said of Jesus, that "he could [in Nazareth] do no mighty work" (Mark 6:5). And why was that? Because of the people's unbelief (see Ether 12:12). They were not in tune with the Spirit. They were not trying to listen with their hearts. They were not trying to be active participants in personally worshipping the Lord in the meeting.

That should help us to see the importance of our praying our way through a meeting, of learning to pray for the speaker. And we especially need to pray for ourselves, that our hearts might be opened, that we might be able to understand what is being said, that we might be able to apply it in the varying circumstances in our lives.

The "King Follett Discourse," a sermon Joseph Smith gave at Brother King Follett's funeral, was one of the Prophet's last public sermons. In his introductory remarks, Joseph made an interesting request: "I want your prayers and faith that I may have the instruction of Almighty God and the gift of the Holy Ghost, so that I may set forth things that are true and which can be easily comprehended by you, and that the testimony may carry conviction to your hearts and minds of the truth of what I shall say. Pray that the Lord may strengthen my lungs, stay the winds, and let the prayers of the Saints to heaven appear, that they may enter into the ears of the Lord of Sabaoth, for the effectual prayers of the righteous avail much. There is strength here, and I verily believe that your prayers will be heard" (*Teachings of the Prophet Joseph Smith,* comp. Joseph Fielding Smith [Salt Lake City: Deseret Book Co., 1976], 342).

For contrast, let me relate this incident: A young boy stood to give a talk in sacrament meeting. He was probably about fourteen years old, and it was his first talk in that setting. He read slowly, deliberately, and without expression from his prepared notes: "Dear brothers and sisters, I am very happy to be here this day to talk to you about the gospel."

One man in the audience was thinking, *That is absolutely the worst talk I have ever heard. I can't believe putting that kid up there. He doesn't know how to talk. He's reading his talk! Why doesn't the bishop get a good speaker? Surely someone else could do a better job — maybe someone like . . . me.* And the man right next to him in the congregation was praying in his heart: "O Heavenly Father, please bless this young man, John. This is the first talk he has ever given. Bless him with thy Spirit. Help him feel the confidence to raise his eyes up from the page and look at us. Help us to convey an acceptance and love to him, that he will feel it, that he will be at ease and be able to truly speak by the Spirit to this congregation."

Just three or four minutes later, John, who had been reading the talk word by word, looked up and said, "Well, brothers and sisters, I don't know too much about what's on this paper, but I do know that the Lord answers your prayers." And then this wonderful youth bore testimony right from his heart about the way the Lord had answered one of his personal prayers.

I believe that the faith exercised by that brother in the audience is what caused that change to occur as John was giving his talk. May I say to you one more time that a good part, I think, of teaching and learning by the Spirit is learning how to pray your way through a meeting.

TEACHER AND LEARNER—A PARTNERSHIP

Let me share another true story, related by a woman who was concerned about the Sunday School class she attended. As you read this example, watch for ways in which the learners and the teacher worked together to help create a learning atmosphere:

"In our new ward my husband and I discovered that the Gospel Doctrine class wasn't very effective. As the teacher talked, some class members read their scriptures; others just kept their heads down. I could tell that this bothered the teacher. Once he even asked, 'Is anybody listening?'

"Soon we learned that a number of people in the ward attended the Gospel Principles class instead of Gospel Doctrine. We heard that the teacher of that class was excellent. We attended the class and found it to be lively, insightful, and rewarding. But walking home from Church one day, we confided to each other that we both felt that what we were doing wasn't quite right. We needed to support our bishop by supporting the teacher he had called to teach us. So we began talking about what we could do to enrich the Gospel Doctrine class. We realized that we had placed all the responsibility for a good class experience on the teacher, as if we were daring him to get our attention and hold our interest.

"We prayed for guidance during the week and went to the Gospel Doctrine class on Sunday with a different spirit. A few minutes into the lesson, my husband asked a question, and the teacher invited other class members to offer answers. A good discussion ensued, to which several class members contributed. Later in the lesson, the teacher made a point that wasn't clear to me, so I asked him to help me understand. He responded by pointing out a scripture that I had never noticed before. Then a sister told a story that reinforced his point, and another class member offered another scripture. We felt the influence of the Spirit in that classroom. The teacher became more relaxed. I could see him gain strength and confidence from our simple gestures of interest and participation. The lesson concluded with a prayer of gratitude and a resounding 'Amen' from the class.

"Since that day most class members have been participating with great interest. Our teacher seems energized by their enthusiasm, and he often expresses gratitude for the support he feels. Sunday School keeps getting better and better" (*Teaching, No Greater Call* [Salt Lake City: The Church of Jesus Christ of Latter-day Saints, 1999], 214–15).

OPEN YOUR EARS

If we hope to learn by the Spirit, we must be able to spiritually hear what the Lord is giving us through the teacher.

I chuckle when I think of a story President Marion G. Romney told some years ago. "Brethren," he said, "I'm really beginning to worry about my wife, Ida. Her hearing is going out on her. It has me really concerned. I'm going home tonight to test her, to see how bad it is."

He went home that night, sat down in his big chair in the living room, and called out in a fairly gentle voice, "Ida, please bring me a glass of water." There was dead silence. So he said a little louder, "Ida, please bring me a glass of water." Again nothing. So this time he loudly said, "Ida, please bring me a glass of water!" She arrived at his side and said, "Why do you keep calling, Marion? I've answered you three times!" Then he understood—it was his own hearing that was going. (See F. Burton Howard, *Marion G. Romney: His Life and Faith* [Salt Lake City: Bookcraft, 1988], 144–45.)

I think of a schoolteacher in Bountiful, Utah, who once told me that she'd lined up all the children in her first-grade class and said: "Now, I've told you guys for the fifth time, 'Do not go out for recess without your boots!' Do you all understand that?" Then, the recess bell rang and it was snowing and muddy outside, and the students began to file out the door. Sure enough, one of the little guys was making a beeline for the door without his boots. The teacher caught him by the collar and said, "Johnny, didn't I tell you to wear your boots to recess?" He looked up at her and said, "Mrs. Bennett, I heard you but I wasn't listening."

If we're not *listening* to the Lord in a meeting, it doesn't do a lot of good to just *hear* the speaker.

Let me briefly recount an experience found in 3 Nephi 11:3–5. Darkness and destruction had signaled the Savior's crucifixion. The terrified Nephites were further startled when, in the midst of their fear, a quiet voice came. It was a small voice, yet it "did pierce them that did hear to the center." You will remember that the voice spoke to them once and they failed to understand it. Twice, "and they understood it not." The third time, the record says, "they did hear the voice, and did open their ears to hear it," and that time they both heard and understood.

That's an incredible story to me. Here someone was speaking from the heavens to them—twice!—and they didn't understand. And then they did something. They opened their ears, and then they understood. Doctrine and Covenants 136:32 explains how to open your ears, your eyes, and your heart: "Let him that is ignorant learn wisdom by humbling himself and calling upon the Lord his God, that his eyes may be opened that he may see, and his ears opened that he may hear."

How do we learn the wisdom that is most important? By humbling ourselves and going to the Lord in prayer—and then by being willing to open our eyes to see and open our ears to hear. Being spiritually open to the Lord is a vital prerequisite to true learning.

SOME SKILLS OF A LEARNER

Now I'd like to discuss some principles I call "learner skills." As I have studied the scriptures, I have identified at least four skills we must develop if we are to understand and learn the gospel and apply it effectively in our lives. Consider how you might apply these four skills in your own teaching and learning settings.

Pray to Understand the Teaching

I am grateful for a principle the Lord teaches in 3 Nephi 20:1. There we read, "And it came to pass that he commanded the multitude that they should cease to pray, and also his disciples." This is the account of the Savior's visit to the Nephites, and in this verse Jesus is telling the multitudes that they should stop praying so he can instruct them. That sounds a little unusual for the Lord to say to stop praying, but consider this important next phrase: "And he commanded them that they should not cease to pray in their hearts."

Now why would he ask them to "not cease to pray in their hearts," or, in other words, to keep praying in their hearts? One possibility is that he wanted them to stay in tune with the Spirit. It also seems that he probably wanted them to humble themselves so they could receive his teaching. The Son of God seems to be saying, in essence, "Continue to pray while I'm teaching you or you won't get it."

In this dispensation the Lord spoke about the responsibility of those who teach the gospel:

> And they shall observe the covenants and church articles to do them, and these shall be their teachings, as they shall be directed by the Spirit.
>
> And the Spirit shall be given unto you by the prayer of faith; and if ye receive not the Spirit ye shall not teach. (D&C 42:13–14.)

Here we see that they are to teach the covenants and Church articles—and they are to do so by the Spirit.

In the Doctrine and Covenants the Lord gives us another witness of this principle:

> And they shall give heed to that which is written, and
> pretend to no other revelation; and they shall pray always
> that I may unfold the same to their understanding. (D&C
> 32:4.)

The Lord in essence is saying that if you don't pray over the
scriptures while you're reading them, you won't understand
them. That's pretty strong counsel. We shouldn't just pick up
the Book of Mormon and start reading it without thought.
We've got to pray over it, and we've got to humble ourselves
before we start praying, or we won't "get it."

And what if we don't pray always? We won't receive what
the Lord has for us. But when we are taught by the Lord, look
what can happen. Joseph Smith wrote of one such occasion:
"We were filled with the Holy Ghost, and rejoiced in the God
of our salvation. Our minds being now enlightened, we began
to have the Scriptures laid open to our understandings, and *the
true meaning and intention of their more mysterious passages
revealed unto us in a manner which we never could attain to previously*" (Joseph Smith, *History of the Church,* 7 vols. [Salt Lake
City: Deseret Book Co., 1980], 1:42–43; emphasis added).

Haven't we all felt that at times—we've been reading and
the Spirit enlightens our minds? It's as if someone just opens a
door and we are filled with understanding. Let's now read
from 2 Corinthians 3:12–16:

> Seeing then that we have such hope, we use great
> plainness of speech:
> And not as Moses, which put a vail over his face, that
> the children of Israel could not stedfastly look to the end
> of that which is abolished:
> But their minds were blinded: for until this day
> remaineth the same vail untaken away in the reading of
> the old testament; which vail is done away in Christ.
> But even unto this day, when Moses is read, the vail
> is upon their heart.

> Nevertheless when it shall turn to the Lord, *the vail shall be taken away.* (Emphasis added.)

The veil Paul was talking about is a veil in one's mind causing him or her to not understand scripture, in this case the Old Testament. Unless your heart is open, the scriptures will be veiled and you will not understand.

How do we get the veil taken away so that the passages will be open to our understanding? We turn to the Lord. Verse 16 teaches clearly that "when [the heart] shall turn to the Lord, the vail shall be taken away."

The things of the Lord can be understood only by the Spirit of the Lord. A person who tries to understand by some other method will not be able to do so.

I have been saddened over the years as I've talked with some people—even some who are close to me—who have said to me in private, "Elder Cook, I've tried to read the scriptures. I just don't get them. I'm sorry. I've tried, but I don't get them. I don't like to read them."

But as we work at applying these skills, the Lord will speak to us every time we pick up the scriptures.

Humble Yourself to Receive True Wisdom

I think this is a real skill of a listener and, of course, for the teacher as well. Let's read from Moroni 10:3:

> Behold, I would exhort you that when ye shall read these things, if it be wisdom in God that ye should read them, that ye would remember how merciful the Lord hath been unto the children of men, from the creation of Adam even down until the time that ye shall receive these things, and ponder it in your hearts.

What should I ponder in my heart? The scriptures in general, yes; but I think the Lord here is telling us something very specific. We are to ponder in our heart *how merciful the Lord has*

been to us. That is a great spiritual key to learning from the Lord.
In Doctrine and Covenants 78:19 we read:

> And he who receiveth all things with thankfulness
> shall be made glorious; and the things of this earth shall
> be added unto him, even an hundred fold, yea, more.

This is the Lord's promise regarding one who will be grateful and who will give thanks for the blessings the Lord has given to him. How much will be added to him? An hundred fold, even more. And why? Because he is grateful. If you will get into the practice of feeling and expressing gratitude to the Lord when you're reading the Book of Mormon, or any of the scriptures—recognizing how merciful he has been to you personally—you will experience the Lord speaking to you more clearly than before, because your heart will be in position to hear.

One of my favorite scriptures is Doctrine and Covenants 136:32, quoted earlier:

> Let him that is ignorant learn wisdom by humbling
> himself and calling upon the Lord his God, that his eyes
> may be opened that he may see, and his ears opened that
> he may hear.

Who is the Lord talking about when he says, "Let him that is ignorant learn wisdom"? He's speaking to all of us, isn't he? When reading the scriptures, I've found it very instructional to not read on when I discover a statement such as this but to instead *ask exactly what the Lord is saying.* For example, where it says, "Let him that is ignorant learn wisdom," I might pause in my reading and think, "How does one obtain wisdom?"

If we asked this question of those in the world, they would most likely advise us to go to the university, study a topic, read a book, do research, or to learn from our experiences.

Interestingly, none of those are the answer the Lord gives to this question. In fact, those methods have little to do with his answer. The Lord says a person learns wisdom by "humbling himself and calling upon the Lord his God, that his eyes may be opened that he may see, and his ears opened that he may hear; for my Spirit is sent forth into the world to enlighten the humble and contrite" (D&C 136:32–33).

Isn't that interesting? The most effective way to get wisdom is to humble yourself. In other words, if you want to be wise with the Lord, if you want to understand in your heart what he is saying to you and be able to hear his voice, the requirement, above all others, is that you humble yourself before God.

And what is the second requirement mentioned in verse 32? The learner should be "calling upon the Lord his God, that his eyes may be opened that he may see, and his ears opened that he may hear." We must, after humbling ourselves, really pray that the Lord will speak into our hearts and that we will perceive his voice and thereby be able to learn from his Spirit.

Be Believing and Harden Not Your Heart

Sometimes members of a congregation may sit in a meeting and critique a talk someone is giving: "Well, I don't think I buy that," or "I don't like that first part," or "I heard that first part—that was pretty good—but I don't think I agree with this second point at all." And that very attitude of being unbelieving, of discounting spiritual instruction without even giving it a chance to work in our hearts, is enough to prevent the Lord's spirit from speaking to us.

Consider this impressive scripture in Mosiah:

And now because of their unbelief they could not understand the word of God; and their hearts were hardened. And they would not be baptized; neither would they join the church. And they were a separate people as to their faith, and remained so ever after, even in their carnal and sinful state; for they would not call upon the Lord their God. (Mosiah 26:3–4.)

It seems to me that the Lord is saying here that if you start on a premise of unbelief, if you have a critical mind, if you are somewhat unbelieving when you're listening, the result is that you'll never get anything from the Spirit. Your unbelief will harden your heart and then you'll be unable to hear the voice of the Lord.

Let's read from Mormon 9:

> Behold, I say unto you that whoso believeth in Christ, doubting nothing, whatsoever he shall ask the Father in the name of Christ it shall be granted him; and this promise is unto all, even unto the ends of the earth. . . . And whosoever shall believe in my name, doubting nothing, unto him will I confirm all my words, even unto the ends of the earth. (Mormon 9:21, 25.)

The Lord here is clearly teaching that he will confirm his words unto the *believing*—those who believe and who doubt not. We cannot doubt, brothers and sisters. If we stand on the neutral line, the doubting line, as the world teaches, then the Lord will not speak to us.

Unbelief causes a hard heart. We all have experience with children, or family members, or students in our Church classes, who listen grudgingly to the gospel or who listen with a hard heart. Our charge, then, as parents and teachers of the gospel, is to help soften their hearts by inviting the Spirit into our teaching. Nothing we could do would be greater than that. Help them be believing and not doubt. Then they will learn from the Lord.

Some people are so intent on challenging what the Lord said in a particular scripture that they become convinced that the Lord is wrong or doesn't know their particular situation, and then their heart becomes hardened.

For example, we often talk in the Church about bearing trials and tribulations, illnesses and sicknesses, the pains and afflictions of life. We all want to learn how to do that better. But

I don't hear very much about how to be healed. But sometimes we're so bent upon all the rest, upon bearing the trial, that we don't focus on the possibility of being healed. I think that's perhaps a reflection of unbelief. We need to trust the simple statement of Jesus: "Whatsoever ye shall ask the Father in my name, which is right, *believing* that ye shall receive, behold it shall be given unto you" (3 Nephi 18:20; emphasis added). The Lord really means that.

I remember a man in a wheelchair once asked President Harold B. Lee, with some bitterness in his voice, "What is this business about the Word of Wisdom? I've kept the Word of Wisdom my whole life. Look at me. I'm crippled, and yet it says in the scriptures that you'll run and not be weary and walk and not faint if you keep the Word of Wisdom. Now tell me, how's that true?" President Lee calmly answered, "My young friend, I didn't say that; the Lord did. The Lord will fulfill his promise. You find out from the Lord what he meant by that."

Apply the Teachings and Repent

I've often thought that if knowledge is not applicable somehow—if we can't apply it in our lives—then it's not of much use to us. Gospel truth must be applied, and that means repentance. If our study of the gospel and our teaching of the gospel are not actively involving us and those we teach in the process of repentance, then something is missing.

If you become one who just *knows* the truths rather than one who seeks to *apply* them, you will not learn or teach by the Spirit and you will not change people's lives, including your own. The Lord gives us truths on the basis of how fast we apply them. If you'll put them into your life—changing self, repenting—the Lord will continue to give you more and more (see 2 Nephi 28:30; Mosiah 12:27; 13:11).

The scriptures are plain in stating that we cannot progress without applying the spiritual knowledge we already possess:

> And they shall remain under this condemnation until
> they repent and remember the new covenant, even the
> Book of Mormon and the former commandments which I
> have given them, *not only to say, but to do* according to that
> which I have written—that they may bring forth fruit
> meet for their Father's kingdom; otherwise there
> remaineth a scourge and judgment to be poured out upon
> the children of Zion. (D&C 84:57–58; emphasis added.)

Again and again, we are counseled to apply the gospel to
our lives—not just to know it but to live it as well.

> And now, behold, I give unto you a commandment,
> that when ye are assembled together ye shall instruct and
> edify each other, *that ye may know how to act* and direct my
> church, *how to act* upon the points of my law and com-
> mandments, which I have given.
> And thus ye shall become instructed in the law of my
> church, and be sanctified by that which ye have received,
> and ye shall *bind yourselves to act* in all holiness before me.
> (D&C 43:8–9; emphasis added.)

I have seen great things happen to Latter-day Saints as they
have faith and apply the gospel in their lives. Some time ago,
for instance, as I presided at a stake conference in eastern
Germany, I met a family I will call the Schmidts. The husband
was a man who prayed sincerely, humbled himself, was believing, and then sought to apply what was said in a Church
meeting.

When I spoke at the conclusion of the Saturday evening
meeting of this stake conference, I told the Latter-day Saints
that it isn't enough to just hear the message, that they have to
be doers of the word as well. I suggested that it wasn't enough
to just go home and say, "That was a wonderful meeting." I
urged them to act on what they had been taught.

In the meeting we had talked about our responsibility to
help bring others to a knowledge of the truthfulness of the

gospel. I asked the members in attendance to take a few minutes in the meeting and to silently pray that the Lord would give them the name of a less-active or nonmember acquaintance whom they might visit on their way home that night and invite to accompany them to conference the next morning. (Parenthetically, I will mention that, having issued that challenge to the Saints in many different meetings for many years, I've seen anywhere from twenty or thirty to even a hundred or more people come to church the next Sunday as a result of these invitations. These are people who never would have come except for the faith of a Latter-day Saint who believed, prayed, humbled himself, and then visited their home the evening before the meeting and invited them to come.)

Let's return to Brother Schmidt, this wonderful German Latter-day Saint. As Brother Schmidt left the meeting, with his two sons at his side, one of the sons said, "Dad, did you pray like Brother Cook asked you to?" Brother Schmidt said he had.

"Whose name came to you?" the son asked. Brother Schmidt answered, "My dad and mom." And the son said, "That's exactly the names that came to me—Grandpa and Grandma." And then the son said to his father, "But we both know they're not going to come. Grandpa is too ill and Grandma won't come without him. Besides, since they're not members of the Church they may not care about conference."

Brother Schmidt couldn't help but agree. Both his parents came to sacrament meeting from time to time, and they had listened to the missionary discussions before, but the father would never commit to be baptized, and the mother decided not to join the Church until her husband did. Now, since Brother Schmidt's father was seriously ill, it seemed even less likely that anything would happen.

"I know," Brother Schmidt said. "It just doesn't seem likely that they will come."

The son said, "But, Dad, we both prayed, and the names

that came to both of us were Grandma and Grandpa. Let's be believing. Let's go invite them."

This faithful brother and his sons arrived at the home of Brother Schmidt's parents, and Brother Schmidt extended the invitation to his parents. To his great surprise, his father said, "Son, can you help me? Do you think that I can get baptized? I want very much to be baptized." Brother Schmidt and his sons were so amazed that they could hardly believe what they were hearing. Brother Schmidt said, "So, Dad, Mom, will you come to the meeting tomorrow?"

They both answered, "We'd be glad to come."

Brother Schmidt brought his father and mother to stake conference the next day. I had a chance to greet them both and express my love to them. I bore my testimony to them and heard the great news of their commitment to be baptized. Six days later, on the next Saturday, Brother Schmidt baptized his aged parents. After his baptism, Grandpa Schmidt called his family together and said, "I am so very happy; now we are all again a family together." And he bore his testimony to his family. Three days after that, on the following Tuesday, he passed away.

A little more than a year later, I had the wonderful experience in the Freiburg Germany Temple of sealing Grandmother Schmidt to her deceased husband and to her parents. This faithful son, who had humbly visited his parents, was also sealed to them that day for time and all eternity. There was a wonderful spirit in the sealing, as these special people were finally joined by temple covenants and by the power of the priesthood.

I bear testimony that this good man, Brother Schmidt, and his sons listened to the Spirit, learned the will of the Lord, and then acted on their knowledge that night. Maybe the one son had a little more faith than the dad, because he really believed that if they prayed, humbled themselves, and then went into action to follow the promptings of the Holy Ghost, success would inevitably follow. I bear testimony that the Spirit really works that way.

What if they had not listened that night? What if they had put off speaking to Brother Schmidt's parents for another week or two? Grandpa Schmidt may have died without having the blessings of baptism in this life.

We, as learners, have to have the Spirit of the Lord with us as much as the teacher does, or we will not be edified. Our role as learners is to be sure that our hearts are prepared to be written upon. Thus we see the great necessity of always praying while we are learning. (That holds true in our academic learning as well. If our young people are praying their way through math and science, they will learn great truths and lessons beyond what their teachers teach.)

SUMMARY

Teaching is much like farming. The farmer cultivates, weeds, fertilizes, plants, irrigates, and provides insect control. But the plant, like the student, must absorb the sun, the dirt, the nutrients needed for growth, and the water, all on its own. The teacher or farmer can do absolutely nothing in that area.

I testify to you that you can learn valuable gospel lessons from every meeting you attend, every talk you hear, and every lesson you listen to, if your heart is right and if you recognize the Lord's Spirit.

QUESTIONS TO PONDER

1. What specific things could you do while in meetings or other settings to better learn directly from the Spirit?

_____

_____

_____

2. How can a student contribute to the success of a class?

_____

_____

_____

3. Why is prayer so important to the learning process? What can you do to improve your prayers as a learner?

_____

_____

_____

4. What can a person specifically do to humble himself or herself in a meeting?

_____

_____

_____

5. Are there some things you need to repent of in order to more clearly hear the voice of the Spirit?

_____

_____

_____

CHAPTER 7

TEACHING YOUR FAMILY
BY THE SPIRIT:
APPLYING THESE PRINCIPLES IN THE HOME

Just as the best meals are home cooked," Elder M. Russell
Ballard has taught, "the most nourishing gospel instruction
takes place at home" ("Feasting at the Lord's Table," *Ensign*,
May 1996, 81).

One afternoon a few years ago, one of my sons (about sixteen years old at the time) came home from school very upset
about things. He was having trouble learning everything he
needed to know for some tests the next day, and some friends
had been giving him a hard time as well. He really felt down.
In his frustration, he began to cause some contention in the
family. My wife and I thought, "Should we get involved?" As
the night wore on, we thought, "No, we'll let it pass. He'll sleep
through this thing and feel better in the morning." We opted
not to get involved, which is difficult sometimes, but I think we
were wise to stay out of the situation that night.

The next morning, however, the problems started again at
breakfast. Because our son was upset, he offended one of his

Note: Some of the stories in this chapter have been adapted from Gene R.
Cook, *Raising Up a Family to the Lord* (Salt Lake City: Deseret Book Co.,
1993), pages 34–74; many other parts are newly added.

sisters, and she began to cry. When breakfast was over, I took him by the arm and said, "Son, come here for a minute." I took him into my bedroom, shut and locked the door, and knelt down. He knelt down as well, still angry.

I did my best to offer a prayer for him: "Heavenly Father, bless my son. He's hurting today. He's had some problems with the family. He's worried about his tests at school." And I expressed my love to him the best I could in that prayer, exercising my faith that the Lord would help him that day if he would humble his heart.

After a few minutes, his heart was humbled, and as soon as the amen was uttered, he said, "Dad, let me pray." In his prayer he asked for forgiveness. He told the Lord that he loved him and that he loved me. He told the Lord he would ask forgiveness of his sister. He even said regarding his upcoming test, "Heavenly Father, please save me." He said he was feeling great stress but that he believed the Lord would help him. After that prayer, a father and a son embraced in great love and, with the Lord as part of the solution, the love between the two of them was enriched a hundredfold.

He went off to school that day, did well on his tests (he got an "A"), and came home on cloud nine, thrilled to tell his mother and me about his success and that he knew the Lord had intervened and helped him. He had no doubt about that. We were thrilled with him—but had to warn him, "Don't think the Lord will bail you out every time. Remember you have to do your part!"

About two weeks later, I was feeling the pressure and strain of having to direct some important meetings and give a couple of talks that day. Again we were sitting at breakfast, and I was not as responsive to some of the children as I should have been. I was feeling about the way my son had felt. I even caused a bit of a problem with one of the children.

After breakfast, my son took me by the arm and said, "Dad,

come with me a minute." Again we went into the bedroom. He shut the door and locked it. He knelt down and I knelt down. Then I heard a good boy offer a prayer for his dad, saying things like, "My dad's really worried. He's got to do some things that he's not had a chance to prepare for as he would have liked to do. He's concerned about his meetings and his talks. Please help him, Heavenly Father. Please inspire him. Help him have more faith. I love him."

It didn't take long for a heart that wasn't as humble as it should have been to be rapidly humbled. And then I offered a prayer of thanksgiving for a good son and asked forgiveness of the Lord. After the prayer there was another hug, and again our love multiplied.

I've often wondered why the love multiplies so in such situations. It is because the Lord is in the situation. It is not just a father or mother giving counsel to a child. But the Lord is in it, and when he is in it, revelation flows and love multiplies.

Well, I went off to work that day and did all the things I had to do. Everything went well. When I pulled into the garage that evening, this same son, who had called ahead to find out what time I had left the office, was waiting for me. When he saw me, he asked, "Well, Dad, how did your day go?" Then, of course, that morning's experience flashed back into my mind, and in gratitude I replied, "Son, this has been a great day. My concerns were unfounded. The Lord did bless me, and I was able to give all my talks."

"I already knew," he said.

"What do you mean?"

"Well, I already knew, Dad. That's the way the Lord does it. I've prayed for you about seventeen times today. I prayed in nearly every class. I prayed when I was at the cafeteria. I even prayed when I was in the bathroom that the Lord would bless you today." And then he added, "I already knew."

I threw my arms around him in love and gratitude—

grateful for a son who would be so faithful, and grateful for a Heavenly Father who would so abundantly bless my son and me.

I've thought much about this incident in relation to teaching by the Spirit. I suspect that neither I nor anyone else could ever teach in words or doctrine all that can be learned in a real experience with the Spirit of the Lord.

How can we teach our children in the home? The best and most powerful way is to teach them by the Spirit. As parents, we can apply the following seven suggestions for inviting the Spirit immediately into any teaching situation:

1. Pray
2. Use the scriptures
3. Bear testimony
4. Use sacred music
5. Express love and gratitude to God and to family members
6. Share spiritual experiences
7. Give priesthood blessings

Because of the importance of these suggestions, they were earlier treated with a focus on teaching in general. Here we review them with emphasis and examples in a family setting.

(Remember, these same suggestions can be used to help couples bring the Spirit into a difficult discussion they are having. And these principles can also be applied by any individual in any situation—if you are feeling discouraged or depressed or frustrated with the challenges of life, you can invite the Spirit to help you by applying one or more of the suggestions in this list. For a full discussion of these seven principles, see chapter 5.)

Rearing and teaching children is often not easy, but we can increase our chances of reaching and touching our children in a positive and powerful way if we will bring the Spirit into all of our teaching opportunities.

THE HOLY GHOST IS THE TEACHER

As we discussed earlier, I think one of the greatest things I know about teaching is that the one taking the role of teacher really is not the teacher. The Lord has said:

> I the Lord ask you this question—unto what were ye ordained? To preach my gospel by the Spirit, even the Comforter which was sent forth to teach the truth. (D&C 50:13–14.)

Who was sent forth to teach the truth to my children? The Comforter. Me? No, the Comforter. I may assist. I may be an instrument in the hands of the Lord to preach and help things along, but the Comforter is the true teacher.

I bear testimony that if we will teach our children to have the Spirit of the Lord, they will be responsive not only to the Lord but to their parents and brothers and sisters as well. Perhaps that is one of the final measures of the degree to which people have the Spirit—they are responsive to the Lord and to their fellowman.

It is one thing to have the Spirit yourself. It is another to be able to use it with other people. When you are ready to teach, make sure the Spirit is there. As the Lord has said, "If ye receive not the Spirit ye shall not teach" (D&C 42:14). Your teaching won't do any good or make any difference if you don't have the Spirit.

As I think about parents teaching their children, sometimes I worry that they're not concerned enough about having the Spirit of the Lord with them all the time while they are teaching. Again, if we don't have the Spirit, we shall not teach—at least not in the Lord's way.

Let us always have a prayer in our hearts as we teach our children. Let us teach our children to also have a prayer in their hearts as we instruct them. Let us seek to help our children have a spiritual experience with the Lord as we teach them. Then they will learn through the Spirit of the Lord.

A parent might offer a simple prayer, such as: "Please instruct me, Heavenly Father. I'm worried about one of my sons. I don't know what to do to soften his heart. Help me." As she prays with a humble heart, the Lord will speak to her and whisper to her something she can now do that she had not thought of before. And as great as the instruction is, the one thing perhaps greater is that she is learning how to receive instruction from the Lord for herself. If we take the Spirit for our guide, we will not be deceived, and we will be enabled to get through these perilous times (see D&C 45:57).

STORIES THAT SHOW HOW TO INVITE THE SPIRIT INTO FAMILY TEACHING SITUATIONS

To help us better understand how to apply these seven principles of inviting the Spirit into our teaching, here are some stories that show the principles in action. As you read these, consider how you can utilize these same approaches in your own home, with your own children—but doing so in your own way, with your own personality. Look for added ways, through these stories, to better teach your family through the Holy Ghost. (And, of course, these stories can also help to illustrate the principles in practice for other teaching purposes as well.)

1. Pray

A few years ago one of our sons, who was then about eight or nine years old, fell in love with a hamster he called Hammy. This son has always loved animals, but he particularly loved Hammy. My son would let him crawl all over his back and up his shirt sleeve and into his shirt. He loved to walk around the house with Hammy in his shirt pocket. He had him sleep by his bed at night in a cage. He loved playing with him when he was doing anything and everything around the house. Hammy became my son's favorite pal.

There were a number of times when Hammy got away from my son and he had to search to find him, but he was always able to do so.

But one day Hammy became lost and we couldn't find him. A full day passed with Hammy missing, and we were afraid he had become stuck somewhere or that he was lost and would die without food and water. The whole family had searched, but the hamster was nowhere to be found. My son left food and water out for him, but it remained untouched.

My son came to me very distraught. "Dad, I know Hammy is going to die. We've looked everywhere, but we can't find him. What'll I do, Dad? What'll I do?"

I said, "Son, you know what to do, don't you?"

He thought about it for a minute and then he said, "Well I've already prayed, Dad. I've already prayed four or five times. So what'll I do now?"

At that moment an inspiration came to me and I said, "Son, I know you have prayed, but have you *really* prayed? Have you told the Lord how much you love Hammy and what he means to you? Have you really pleaded with the Lord, with a humble heart, that he will tell you where your hamster is? Have you done it with all your heart?"

He thought about that for a minute, and then he said, "Nope, I haven't prayed that way, Dad." And then he disappeared. About five minutes later he came running up the stairs with his hamster in his hand, shouting, "I've got the hamster! I've found Hammy!"

Then he told me that he'd gone back downstairs, bowed down on his knees, and pleaded with the Lord in a very simple child's prayer, explaining the problem. "Heavenly Father, Hammy's lost. If we don't find him pretty quick, he's going to die. He's my best friend. Please, please help me find him."

Then, when he opened his eyes, Hammy was sitting right there on the carpet in front of him. My son said, "Dad, it looked to me like he was praying too."

If the Lord will help a little child when he prays for help in finding his hamster, won't he help us when we humbly pray for help in receiving his Spirit? Remember:

> The Spirit shall be given unto you by the prayer of faith; and if ye receive not the Spirit ye shall not teach. (D&C 42:14.)

This applies to teaching in the home as well as anywhere else. Let us offer a prayer of faith that we may receive the Spirit, that that Spirit will be present and active in all our teaching. Let us pause in the middle of the action, check in with the Lord, and give him an opportunity to speak to us, to inspire us, to help us. Let us watch for special teaching moments that present themselves as they did in this experience—and then let us take advantage of these opportunities in teaching our children.

2. Use the Scriptures

One morning while we were living in Germany, my wife was ill and my son had gone to seminary on a very early morning train. I found myself having family scripture study with just my daughter, who was eleven or twelve years old. We sat down on the couch to begin. I opened up my triple combination, and at that instant my daughter said, "Wait! Wait! Wait!" I said, "What?" She said, "Do that again." I said, "What?" She said, "Open your book again, close it, and open it again." Then she took the book and opened and closed it the way she had suggested I do.

Then she said, "Dad, I want you to know that is my favorite sound."

I was somewhat taken aback and said, "I don't follow what you mean, honey."

And she said, "That cracking, opening of your book—I have heard that for almost all of my life, early in the morning, for scripture study. That is my favorite sound."

When I realized what she was really saying, I was really touched to think that of all the things my daughter had heard through the years, that was the sound that topped them all. She felt that hearing the triple combination open up in the morning, when we would read the scriptures, pray together as a family, and feel the Spirit of the Lord, was truly her favorite thing to hear.

That morning, unlike other mornings where I felt that I was the one trying to teach my daughter by the Spirit, through the scriptures, she really taught me.

I know when we read or speak the words the Lord has given us in the holy scriptures, the Spirit of the Lord comes. If you will do it in humility, the moment you pick up the passages and start to read them, the Lord will speak through you in power, and the Spirit will be conveyed to those who are listening.

The scriptures are the words of the Lord to us, and the Spirit of the Lord will speak through them to all—both young and old. If we use the scriptures to teach our families, the very words of the Lord will reach their hearts. This is a core element of teaching by the Spirit: to use scripture so that the Lord's words will be conveyed directly and boldly, without excuse, to others.

I remember once when two of our daughters were coming into their teen years and were beginning to feel pressure from their peers to dress a little more like some of the young women of the world. Some were telling them they should wear more makeup, more jewelry, more worldly clothing. We were reading the scriptures one morning when the subject came up. I think by inspiration we just happened to be reading in the Book of Mormon in the words of Isaiah:

> Because the daughters of Zion are haughty, and walk
> with stretched-forth necks and wanton eyes, walking and
> mincing as they go, and making a tinkling with their
> feet—therefore the Lord will smite with a scab the crown
> of the head of the daughters of Zion, and the Lord will
> discover their secret parts. (2 Nephi 13:16–17.)

We immediately saw that these passages were not directed
to daughters of the world but as a warning to the daughters of
Zion, to faithful female members of the Church. The Lord
spoke of how in the last days many would be tempted to do
just what some were suggesting to my daughters that they
do—namely, to dress in a more worldly way.

Isaiah continues:

> In that day the Lord will take away the bravery of
> their tinkling ornaments, and cauls [hairnets], and round
> tires like the moon [ornaments like a crescent moon]; the
> chains and the bracelets, and the mufflers [veils]; the bon-
> nets, and the ornaments of the legs, and the headbands,
> and the tablets, and the ear-rings; the rings, and nose jew-
> els; the changeable suits of apparel, and the mantles, and
> the wimples, and the crisping-pins; the glasses [transpar-
> ent garments], and the fine linen, and hoods, and the veils.
> (2 Nephi 13:18–23.)

Evidently the Lord is not pleased with those who go too far
in adorning their bodies. The Lord is surely not suggesting that
we go to the extreme of not doing anything to adorn ourselves,
but he is giving a great caution about going too far, about
beginning to dress in the ways of the world.

This underscores a great principle that is taught to the missionaries and that probably applies well to teaching this principle to our sons and daughters: *There should never be anything
about you—the way you speak or especially your appearance—that
comes over stronger than the real you.* In other words, we want
people to know us and love us for being ourselves, not for

"I Even Remain Alone" by Walter Rane
from the book *By the Hand of Mormon*

2004 GOSPEL DOCTRINE READING SCHEDULE

1. 1 Nephi 13:38–41;
   19:23; 2 Nephi 5:21–22;
   27:22; 29:6–9;
   Mormon 8:26–41;
   Ether 5:2–4; Moroni
   1:4; 10:3–5;
   Doctrine and Covenants
   10:45–46; 20:8–12;
   84:54–58
2. 1 Nephi 1–7
3. 1 Nephi 8–11;
   12:16–18; 15
4. 1 Nephi 12–14
5. 1 Nephi 16–22
6. 2 Nephi 1–2
7. 2 Nephi 3–5
8. 2 Nephi 6–10
9. 2 Nephi 11–25
10. 2 Nephi 26–30
11. 2 Nephi 31–33
12. Jacob 1–4
13. Jacob 5–7
14. Enos, Jarom, Omni,
    Words of Mormon
15. Mosiah 1–3
16. Mosiah 4–6
17. Mosiah 7–11
18. Mosiah 12–17
19. Mosiah 18–24
20. Mosiah 25–28; Alma 36
21. Mosiah 29; Alma 1–4
22. Alma 5–7
23. Alma 8–12
24. Alma 13–16
25. Alma 17–22
26. Alma 23–29
27. Alma 30–31
28. Alma 32–35
29. Alma 36–39
30. Alma 40–42
31. Alma 43–52
32. Alma 53–63
33. Helaman 1–5
34. Helaman 6–12
35. Helaman 13–16
36. 3 Nephi 1–7
37. 3 Nephi 8–11
38. 3 Nephi 12–15
39. 3 Nephi 17–19
40. 3 Nephi 16; 20–21
41. 3 Nephi 22–26
42. 3 Nephi 27–30; 4 Nephi
43. Mormon 1–6; Moroni 9
44. Mormon 7–9
45. Ether 1–6
46. Ether 7–15
47. Moroni 1–6
48. Moroni 7–8;10

Deseret Book | DeseretBook.com
1-800-453-4532

external adornments used to attract attention or perhaps even motivate some unrighteous feelings in those who might be influenced by us.

As we read these passages that morning and, as parents, bore testimony to the truthfulness of the principles, we could see that the message reached the hearts of our girls. They asked a number of questions: "What about this? What about that?" As we worked through those questions as a family, a standard evolved about what the Lord expects of a righteous young woman in properly adorning herself. The standard was not our standard, but it was based on a standard given in the scriptures. In other words, it was the Lord's standard.

What made this experience so powerful was the fact that had it been just our standard, we would later have had to enforce it with more specific rules and perhaps to discuss it frequently with our children. (And we have done some of that over the years.) But what impressed us most was the fact that the Lord himself, through his Spirit, reached the hearts of our daughters that morning. He placed in them a value, a standard, a level of expectation, that did not come from their parents. It came from the Lord. Thus, they accepted it as their own and lived it from that day forward.

Thanks be to the scriptures. Thanks be to the Lord for his words that are so imbued with his Spirit. You will face nothing in life for which the basic principles are not found in the scriptures. The key is to understand them and to share them with your family. You will thereby be able to better teach by the Spirit.

May I restate again that the goal isn't just finding knowledge or clarification of a principle in the scriptures. The goal is to come to the added testimony that can come with the scriptures, causing the teaching to come by the Spirit, through a good parent, to reach the heart of the child and change his heart.

Sometimes the child will not respond as quickly as illustrated above. Sometimes one of your children might need to prayerfully consider something and weigh it over a period of time in order to gain a true understanding. Yet, once again, if the parent teaches the principle by the Spirit and if the child is taught how to receive an answer from the Lord by praying about it himself, he will then obtain from the Lord the truth in his own heart, which will change his behavior.

In the Book of Mormon, Alma, the great high priest, was greatly concerned about the apostasy of the Zoramites, some of the less-active members of his day. As he pondered what he should do, he received this great understanding from the Lord:

> As the preaching of the word had a great tendency to lead the people to do that which was just—yea, it had had more powerful effect upon the minds of the people than the sword, or anything else, which had happened unto them—therefore Alma thought it was expedient that they should try the virtue of the word of God. (Alma 31:5.)

The preaching of the word of the Lord affected their minds and changed their hearts; nothing had a more powerful effect on the people. If parents can adopt that approach, making sure that their children are exposed regularly to the words of the Lord, many of their problems will be solved in the children's early years and will never come up later. President Boyd K. Packer explained the power that comes to our children (and ourselves!) as we study the doctrines of the Lord:

"True doctrine, understood, changes attitudes and behavior," he said. "The study of the doctrines of the gospel will improve behavior quicker than a study of behavior will improve behavior" ("The Twelve Apostles," *Ensign*, Nov. 1986, 17).

3. Bear Testimony

Sister Susan L. Warner, who served as second counselor in the Primary general presidency, told the following story:

"I know a grandfather who, at a recent family gathering in

the mountains, took his grandchildren for a walk. As they came to a clearing in the trees, he invited the young children to sit down on a log while he told them about a 14-year-old boy named Joseph Smith, who wanted to ask Heavenly Father some questions that were troubling him. The grandfather explained that the boy Joseph went to a grove of trees near his home to pray, having faith that God would answer him. The grandchildren quietly listened, but four-year-old Johnny, who often has difficulty sitting still, could not contain himself. He blurted out, 'I've heard that story before.'

"The grandfather told of Joseph's sincere prayer and how it was answered with a glorious visitation from Heavenly Father and His Son, Jesus Christ. As he finished, little Johnny grabbed his grandfather's hand and said, 'That was a good testimony, Grandpa.' He loved hearing the story again.

"Though the grandfather had repeated this sacred account many times throughout his life, he said, 'Never did the Spirit of the Lord bear stronger witness than when I bore my testimony of Joseph Smith to my own grandchildren.' The grandfather and the children had felt the witness of the Holy Ghost" ("Bear Record of Him," *Ensign*, Nov. 1998, 67).

At times parents forget the great power that is found in bearing testimony to their children. When they do so humbly they will be speaking by the Spirit, and thus they will be teaching by the Spirit. Sometimes we're more of a mind to try to convince them logically that something is right, such as paying tithing, keeping the Sabbath day holy, coming in at a reasonable hour in the evening, being kind to their friends, and so on. At times we can describe things logically and teach them to our family and they are accepted. But many times that is not the case. One of the greatest spiritual tools the Lord has given us for influencing others, including our children, is the power of our own testimony. If fathers and mothers will speak by the power of the Holy Ghost in love and testimony to their children, the message will reach their hearts and can change them.

As we have noted before, Alma taught that when he saw the "pride" and "contentions" among his people, he bore "down in pure testimony against them" (Alma 4:19), knowing the great potential power of such an approach.

Children as well as adults can be proud or angry or contentious and thus repel the Spirit of the Lord. But a parent's testimony can help dispel such negative attitudes.

I had an experience with one of my sons when he was about eight years old that further illustrates the power of this approach. He was studying math and had learned nearly all of his pluses and minuses, passing them off with me. But after a while he got discouraged and quit. I let him decide what to do, thinking that after a while he would come back and finish them up. But he never returned. Finally, some days later, I "laid down the law" and told him that we had to solve this problem that had come between us. He was a little hard-hearted and didn't want to do it. I had him sit on a chair for a while, and that still didn't help to humble him.

Finally, I realized I was approaching him in the wrong way, so he and I went into the bedroom and prayed together. That softened his heart about halfway. Then I told him he ought to stay in the bedroom and pray and find out what the Lord wanted him to do, to listen for the voice of the Lord. Somewhat to my surprise, instead of staying there a minute or two, he stayed there on his knees ten or fifteen minutes. When I finally went back to see how he was doing, he said the Lord had told him by the Spirit that he should do his math and that he would obey that voice and do it even though he didn't want to.

I was thrilled to hear that he had had a real experience with the Lord—that he had actually heard the Lord's voice and recognized it. He and I went to tell his mother about it. Then we spent some time studying, and he passed off the first of three tests on his pluses. He couldn't pass off his minuses that day, but a couple of days later he did.

This whole episode seemed to turn on the impression that I should take my son into our room to pray. The thought was clear that if I could do that and humble his heart, then he would respond and learn his math tables. But it had to be because he wanted to, not just because I wanted him to. The Spirit had to touch him for that to occur—my words were not enough. The whole issue began to turn when, on bended knee, I bore testimony and told him that I knew the Lord would help him if he would have faith. The words were carried from my heart to his, and he humbled himself and stayed there in the room, praying until his heart was fully humbled. If we can remember to use such spiritual tools in dealing with our children, we will have much more of an impact upon them.

There is another valuable way we can invite the Spirit through testimony, and that is to encourage our children to gain a testimony for themselves of the truthfulness of what we say.

More than once my children have protested family rules, saying things like, "Well, why can't we stay out until one or two o'clock? Everybody else does it. Why do we have this rule to be home by midnight when you're sixteen or seventeen?" Probably every parent is familiar with such arguments. And I've often not known how to answer such questions very well. When I try to explain or tell them my reasons, it has never worked very effectively. But here is an approach that has worked. I've said, "Well, the reason we have that rule is that your mom and I have prayerfully considered it and we feel like that's what the Lord would say. Now if you want to know for yourself, go ask him. You can go confirm that what we've told you is true."

It's been amazing to me that in the instances when children have really done that, when they have prayed about such issues, the Lord has answered them. Either he has said, "Sustain your parents in this and obey what they have determined," or, many times he has given them the same witness that we received on that particular thing. Then they have come back to us and have said, "Okay, we can handle that rule. We think that what you have decided really is from the Lord." In the process, then, the Lord has given them a new heart, as it were, because we referred them back to him.

4. Use Sacred Music

Music really is the language of heaven. The Lord is able to teach us by the Spirit in many ways, not only through individuals, as we have illustrated many times in this book, but it can be directly from his Spirit to ours or as a result of the wonderful medium of music.

My wife tells an interesting account of how she received her first testimony, and how in reality she was taught directly by the Spirit through music. She has recorded the following experiences:

"One of my first recollections of ever being taught by the Spirit, or having felt the Spirit, as it taught and witnessed to me of the truthfulness of the gospel, was when I was a young girl around the age of eight or nine. I was attending a branch in Superior, Arizona, where, at that time, my father was not a member of the Church. My mother took us to the little branch where she served, in turn, as the ward pianist, Relief Society president, Primary president, and so forth.

"In Primary, one day, we sang 'Called to Serve.' I vividly remember standing and singing that song with the Spirit filling my soul and witnessing to me as I sang the words—'Called to serve Him, heav'nly King of glory.' It just burned in my heart that the Church was true and that Heavenly Father really did know who I was and that he loved me. This experience was a witness of the Spirit. It testified to me of the truthfulness of the gospel. It helped me to understand how the Spirit speaks to me and how he speaks to all of us. It may have been my first experience with the way teaching by the Spirit works. I had been taught by the Spirit!

"Some three or four years later, after we had moved to Mesa, Arizona, the bishop in our ward wanted to use the Young Women as part of the Sunday School music appreciation time. This was a time for singing and for practicing the hymns. The bishop called four or five of us young girls into his office and called us to be the Sunday School choristers. We were to rotate and take turns leading the music. In order to do that, we were to go to a Brother Smith's home, where he taught us how to lead the music properly. As he taught us, he impressed on us that we had to memorize every word, every verse of each song. So when it was my turn, if I were to lead the song, 'Lead, Kindly Light,' I was to memorize every word of that hymn. He taught us that if we were to do that, we would feel confident as we stood before the congregation. He also told us to pray so we could sing the hymn to the Lord with the people.

"When it was my turn I found myself standing there looking into the faces of the Saints and singing, 'I know that my Redeemer lives. . . . He lives to wipe away my tears.' I felt those words so strongly they just burned in my heart, that he truly does live and that he was there to comfort me and to wipe away my tears. I had a similar experience in singing 'Come, Come, Ye Saints,' and 'Jesus, Savior, Pilot Me.' With any one of those songs, the words were truly a testimony to me.

"And it was true what Brother Smith had said: that we could look out into their faces, we could smile, we could pray to be able to sing the hymn to the Lord, we could encourage them to sing because we had the confidence of knowing the words. I felt this was a true blessing to me because from then on as I was doing my dishes or hanging out the clothes, I was memorizing the hymns from the hymnbook. What a wonderful blessing to me and later to my own family. I don't know how many hymns I memorized at that point, but there must have been twenty or thirty. I felt the words burn in my soul and witness to me, even more than before, the truthfulness of the gospel and how the Spirit speaks to me.

"I learned even more—that the words of the hymns are prayers. As I would sing, I felt I was singing to my Heavenly Father, and I felt his love and his assurance and how much he cared for me. I learned sometime later of the scripture in Doctrine and Covenants 25:12 where the Lord is speaking to Emma Smith about the sacred hymns of the Church. He says, 'For my soul delighteth in the song of the heart; yea, the song of the righteous is a prayer unto me, and it shall be answered with a blessing upon their heads.' I truly felt as I sang that these were prayers unto Heavenly Father, and that gave me a foundation for my testimony that has carried me through to this day.

"This first testimony was a wonderful prelude to further faith that has come to me through the years. This experience has helped me teach my own children how the Lord can teach us by the Spirit through music. The Lord truly does have many miraculous ways to teach us."

Sister Cook also relates this more recent experience where she saw the teaching power of music:

"Not long ago I was asked to teach the first lesson of the year to the Relief Society sisters in our ward, from the teachings of Joseph F. Smith. The name of the lesson was 'I Know That My Redeemer Lives.' I felt so inadequate about teaching, in the first place, and then to teach on this particular subject added even more to my concern. I struggled within myself to be prepared to feel the Spirit as I taught, and to also convey the Spirit to the class.

"I prayed over this lesson and the material in the manual. I prayed, studied, and pondered the lesson over and over. I read the scriptures that I felt were appropriate for the topic, and yet I still felt something lacking. It just wasn't coming together, and it was already Saturday—the day before the lesson was to be given.

"At one point, while I was pondering again the message and the material at home, my son sat down to practice the piano. Because music is such a strong and vital part of my life in the gospel, when he started playing 'I Believe in Christ' with great feeling, I immediately stopped what I was doing. I paused, and as I listened, I felt the Spirit witness to me that the sisters needed to hear this song as part of my lesson. I needed to have my son play it, and as he played I needed to have the sisters read and ponder the words of the music. I felt the Spirit teaching me and witnessing to me that that was what I needed to do. I knew I had been taught by the Spirit. Because I was so touched by this experience my son was quick to agree that he would play.

"During my lesson the next morning, when my son started playing that hymn, a truly incredible spirit flooded the room. This was a witness to all of us that the Savior truly lives, that he is our Redeemer. It was what I needed—we all needed it. The sisters did their part in learning by the Spirit—they were wiping their tears as my son played. It was a magnificent experience and a witness and testimony to me of the influence that music can have in our teaching. How I appreciate the music of the Church as a means for conveying the Spirit! The Lord that day taught us all by the Spirit."

Some have asked, "How can I effectively use music in the home to set a spiritual mood and invite the Spirit into our home?" Several answers come to mind:

• Our family sings before family prayer—usually just a verse or two and almost always from memory.

• We sing before scripture reading and during family home evenings.

- We have a number of tapes of spiritual music that we really like. Many times, especially on Sunday or early in the morning, we'll play them to set the spirit in the home. Sometimes when there has been a little contention or some problems, my wife turns on some of that music, and it seems to calm everyone.

- As parents we have found it most enjoyable for all if Dad or Mom sings to the children after they have prayed and are in bed ready to go to sleep. We've always sung to the younger ones. Our older girls even enjoyed that special attention into their teenage years.

- As a young missionary, I had a number of discouraging days, but I learned a great lesson and now I have a lot fewer of those days. What I have learned is that I used to wait until I was discouraged before using music or some of the other spiritual tools. As I got a little older I thought, "Why wait? Why go into the valley of despair before trying to be happy? Why not use those things every day and thus avoid discouragement altogether?"

Music can have a great impact on our families if we use it appropriately. As you use music in the spirit of worship, it will become a prayer to the Lord (see D&C 25:12), helping you, your spouse, and your children to soften your hearts and be taught by the Spirit of the Lord.

I've always been impressed by what Jesus and his apostles did before he went out to suffer in the Garden of Gethsemane: "When they had sung an hymn, they went out into the mount of Olives" (Matthew 26:30). I'm sure the Lord received great comfort from that hymn. Could not our families obtain the same benefit?

Also, great teaching comes from singing the songs of Zion. It has been a great blessing for me to learn songs like "I Am a Child of God" and "Teach Me to Walk in the Light."

If children were to hear the songs of Zion sung at home and

learned to sing them themselves while getting dressed or taking a shower, it would surely remove a lot of negativity from our homes and replace it with the Spirit of the Lord. There is nothing quite like a good hymn to discourage discouragement.

Let us, then, let music ring in our homes—good, wholesome music that will lift the spirits of all and lift our hearts to the Lord. Thereby we will invite the Spirit of the Lord to be with us. The hymns of the Church are part of the language of heaven and thus can empower us to both listen and teach by the Spirit.

5. Express Love and Gratitude to God and to Family Members

Express love openly for God and to the members of your family, and the Spirit will be felt profoundly (see John 13:34–35; 1 Nephi 11:21–23; Moroni 7:47–48). It is impossible to stand up and express genuine love for the Lord and not have the Spirit of the Lord come upon you. It's impossible to humbly count your blessings and not have the Spirit of the Lord come to you. It's impossible to express your love sincerely to one of your family members or to your spouse and not have the Spirit of the Lord come. If you want to bring the Spirit of the Lord into your home, you must learn yourself and teach your children how to regularly express love and gratitude to God and to one another. Love has tremendous power.

Let me illustrate this principle with an incident that occurred between my daughter and me (she was about twelve years old at the time) when I was about to leave for a stake conference. I was talking with her one night, and after she had said her prayers, I asked her what she prayed about.

She said, "What do you mean, Dad?"

"What do you pray about?" I responded. "Now that you're older, you say your prayers silently, and I don't get to hear them anymore."

She replied, "Well, I always tell Heavenly Father how much I love him. Not just sometimes—I always tell him. He's given me so many blessings. I'm very thankful for all my blessings."

Then she said, "Dad, do you have to go to conference again tomorrow?"

I told her I did.

She said, "Oh, it breaks my heart to have you leave. It's hard for me to see you go every week. Do you have to go again?"

I told her that I did, and I explained why. She threw her arms around my neck and expressed her love to me, telling me how much she would miss me. I found it hard to make her understand why I had to go.

I finally determined that the best way to help her understand was to pray with her. I asked her to offer prayer that I would be safe on the journey, and she did so, expressing love for me and faith in the Lord that I would be protected. Then I offered a prayer in thanksgiving for such a wonderful daughter. The Spirit of the Lord came in abundance, and our love was greatly increased as a result of that small experience together. Through the prayer, and through my expression of love and gratitude, the Spirit taught her what she needed to know, and the blessing of understanding I sought for her was granted. Love honestly expressed by me and felt by her was conveyed by the Spirit; and thus we both were taught by the Spirit.

The next day as I flew to San Francisco, I thought, "What a power love is, especially the love between a father and a daughter." The Spirit seemed to impress upon me how much I loved my daughter and what a good girl she was. Her heart was always softened to spiritual things. She was always quick to help others. I thought what a wonderful wife and mother she would one day be. I thought of how much I wanted to bless her, how there wasn't anything I wouldn't do to help her stay close to our Father in Heaven. How strongly I felt the Spirit that morning! Yes, when one is filled with love, the Spirit comes in abundance.

It is most impressive to understand that when sincere love or gratitude is expressed, the Spirit of the Lord comes in abundance. Let us be filled with love in our families and thus be filled with the Spirit of the Lord.

6. Share Spiritual Experiences

In your family, when you are prompted to do so, share a spiritual experience. Sometimes we might not give our best effort in teaching because, after all, who is listening? "Just our family." But who is more important?

Instead of just teaching principles or even telling our children what to do, we can tell them about a spiritual experience and help them relate it to the challenge they are facing. This will have much more of an impact in changing their hearts. If we do this, we will influence them for righteousness' sake because the Spirit of the Lord is with us.

I've also found that many experiences with my family have been of great benefit to others, and I believe strongly in recording in some detail my key experiences week after week. I have learned, as have many others, that if I do not record them when they occur, the impact of the experiences or the feelings that attended them are soon lost. However, if I record them and remember them, I can use them to help others.

Here's an example of how sharing a personal spiritual experience made a difference in a person's life. During a stake conference in the Midwest, I learned that the mission president and his wife were bringing an investigator to the meeting. She had taken the missionary lessons a number of times and had read much about the Church, but she just could not make the decision to be baptized. As a professional psychologist, she was having trouble with the intellectual decision about whether the

Church was true. The president and his wife asked if I would talk with her.

Before the Sunday meeting, I was shaking hands with people in the congregation, and I talked with this woman for a few minutes. She seemed to be one of those people who have a testimony but just don't realize it. I asked her to listen carefully during the conference, suggesting that the Lord would tell her in her heart as well as in her mind what she ought to do, and that she should then be courageous enough to follow those promptings.

During my talk, I discussed the need to trust one's feelings, and I told a story about a scientist I had met who had wanted to calibrate everything in a test tube, so to speak, before accepting it as true. However, he deeply loved his wife and children, and he finally realized that this truth of the heart was greater than anything he might learn through the scientific method. I said that there are two ways to learn—by the mind and by the heart. Each is needful and important, but in spiritual matters, we need to be sure to give place to the feelings the Spirit gives us, especially as they are manifest in the heart.

Six weeks later I received a letter from her. She wrote: "My greatest stumbling block in getting closer to the Church is my fearfulness in trusting my feelings as a valid basis for a decision. I respect the commitment of baptism too much to join the Church lacking conviction and confirmation on which to build the foundation of a testimony and solid membership. I sincerely desire to believe. I have fasted and prayed and read the scriptures. I attend meetings, keep the commandments and Word of Wisdom, and pay tithing. I feel weary and frustrated, and I know the deficit is in me. Although this is not one of those decisions one can intellectualize entirely, or get swept away by nice feelings or programs or friendly people, it is hard for me to know how to discern the appropriate devotion and cause of action.

"This is the most important decision I will ever make, and I feel terribly accountable and rather inadequate. This circumstance makes me feel very humble and reliant upon God for help—which is probably good.

"Regardless of any decision I eventually make, I am grateful for what I've learned. Whether or not I join the LDS church I will always feel kindly toward it because I have been given much by it and because of it. Thank you."

As I read her letter, I thought, "I'll call her this week sometime, or maybe write her a letter." But as I was working at home that morning, the impression came a couple of times that I should call her, and that I should do it now. I called the mission president, got her phone number, and called her home only to reach her answering machine. I thought, "Well, she's probably at work, so I'll just leave my phone number." Why, then, had I received those urgent impressions?

To my surprise, just two minutes later, she returned my call. She said, "I just got home a minute or so after you left your message."

I thanked her for her letter and said I had felt I should call and talk with her about her feelings.

She told me that it wasn't just by chance that I had called, and she was very touched by the fact that I would call. She said, "You wouldn't have known this, but I've been somewhat discouraged about all of this, and in the past couple of weeks have been somewhat turned away, almost deciding I ought not go in the direction of becoming a member of the Church. At least I've been discouraged about it and have about determined to just forget it all. I was thinking those thoughts even this very morning. It's interesting that you would call me right now when I needed something."

Her greatest concern seemed to center in her inability to trust her feelings as a valid basis for a decision. It was evident as I interviewed her on the phone that she was morally clean, keeping the Word of Wisdom, and even paying tithing. She was obedient to the commandments. She just didn't know for sure that it was all true or at least did not know how to obtain a confirmation so she would know that she knew it was true.

I talked with her about the times she had felt the Spirit as a swelling in the breast (see Alma 32:28), as a burning in the bosom (see D&C 9:8), and as a feeling of peace (see D&C 6:22–23), and about the need to trust in the Spirit and thereby receive its fruits and the witness she lacked (see D&C 11:12–14).

I had previously discussed with my wife a couple of stories that I might share to help this woman understand how to trust her feelings in faith, and I decided to tell her about one of my sons.

This son had decided to go to college, but he didn't have a job to support himself while he was there. Nevertheless, he went in pure faith that he would obtain employment, trusting that the Lord would deliver something up. As the days passed, though, nothing came through. Finally, out of funds, he called to tell us he would have to come home. Our family fasted and prayed for him, and within twenty-four hours of the time he was going to leave, he had three job offers. He was greatly blessed to work at two of the three jobs. I told this woman that such things happen through faith, after our faith has been tested and tried.

I challenged her not to do what anyone else told her to do, that we would never want her to feel pressured to be baptized, but that she now needed to go to the Lord and humbly pray again for direction as to what he would have her do. I promised her in the name of the Lord that if she would do that, she would receive the impression in her heart and mind of what she ought to do, and that she ought to then be spiritually mature enough to act on those impressions given by the Spirit.

The next day in my office, I received a message from the

mission president that the woman had asked for baptism the coming Saturday.

During our phone conversation, this good sister and I discussed many of the principles of how to gain a testimony. But I think it was the story of my son at college—a story I had written in my journal so I would not forget it—that really helped her understand what she needed to do.

Seek to have spiritual experiences. Then record them. And then pray during your time of need that the appropriate ones will come back to your mind to help people in need. Spiritual experiences have great impact upon the soul. Share them as prompted by the Spirit (see D&C 50:21–22; Luke 10:25–37; Acts 26:1–32). Sharing spiritual experiences truly will empower you to more effectively teach by the Spirit. As we share such experiences, the Lord can use them to reach the hearts of others.

7. Give Priesthood Blessings

One final example of how the Lord can teach us through his Spirit is through priesthood blessings. Sometimes we are very frustrated with life and having difficult times handling certain situations. The Lord is very capable of speaking to us through the Spirit, if we will listen by the Spirit, and he will give us added instruction for our well-being. We can also use priesthood blessings, when appropriate, to help bring the Spirit into a private teaching setting (such as in a home), to open hearts to the words of truth we have to share.

My wife relates this special experience with a priesthood blessing:

"In 1985 we were called to go to Mexico City, where my husband was to preside over the Mexico/Central America Area. When we were called, I was four or five months pregnant, and we already had a large family. My husband was very, very ill with various health problems. He had just had two different operations and was barely out of the hospital.

Nevertheless, we accepted the call. We were very excited about the opportunity of living in Mexico and of giving our children another mission experience.

"Our new daughter was born on August 10, and we left for Mexico City approximately two weeks later, in time to get the children enrolled in school. When we arrived in Mexico City, we lived in a home that the Church provided for us. It was wonderful, but it needed to be prepared for our large family of eight children. It seemed we had workers coming in and out of the house for days on end, making repairs to the kitchen or bathroom. It was one thing after another. I was still adjusting to the new baby, and it was a very strenuous and difficult time for me.

"We tried very hard to settle into a new environment. Our children, many of whom did not speak Spanish, needed a lot of help to deal with their new world. My husband really helped me by taking them to be enrolled in school. This was difficult for him—besides still dealing with his health problems, he was stopped by the police twice as he was trying to get to the school. My personal stress level was at its limit.

"One morning I awakened and went into the kitchen to prepare breakfast for the family and tried to light the oven. I had not had any previous experience with a gas oven. I turned on the gas and lit the match—but I had left the gas on too long, and a huge bolt of flames singed my hair, my eyebrows, and my eyelashes, and scared me to death. I went screaming out of the kitchen. I was completely at my wits' end. I ran into the back room to find my husband and ask him if he would please give me a blessing. I told him that I had just *had* it. I told him I couldn't handle the stress from being up all night with the baby and with all the kids and the workers during the day—and now this. My coping ability had just come to an end.

"We went into the bedroom and there my husband placed his hands on my head. I immediately felt the Spirit enter my soul and begin to calm my nerves. As he spoke the words of the blessing, I felt love and peace come into my heart. It settled me down, and he spoke words of hope from the Lord, promising that even these problems would pass away. I clearly remember how wonderful I felt after that blessing, how the Spirit spoke to my heart and told me that the Lord understood my challenges! The Lord felt my need for him, and through this priesthood blessing he spoke to me, expressing his love and encouragement and confidence that he would be with me! I did feel that peace and assurance that things would work out.

"After that, things did go better. The problems did not all go away at once, but I was able to cope and handle challenges in the home, the children's difficulties at school, and everything else, even with my husband's constant traveling. The stress and pressures were alleviated. The blessing gave me the hope and the witness that the Lord truly was there. He taught me by the Spirit that I was his daughter, that he loved me, and that he would *always* be there for me. I knew these things before, but that priesthood blessing taught them to me anew. I love the way the Lord can teach us and help us to learn from his wonderful Spirit."

What a blessing it is to have the priesthood in the home, either in a worthy father or a worthy son. Those families who have neither can still turn to a relative, or to a friend who is a home teacher, priesthood leader, quorum leader, or neighbor. Using the priesthood and its ordinances in your home is another way to invite the Spirit of the Lord to help you in teaching your family.

Children learn to ask for blessings if they see their parents having blessings. They learn to ask for blessings if parents, through faith, teach them the importance of having a blessing. Then the Lord will help them more because of their faith. If your children can see the results of a priesthood blessing, you will not have to tell them to ask for one.

When we returned to the United States from living in Mexico, one of my daughters was having difficulty adjusting because she could not find a friend. She didn't feel close to anyone, and she didn't feel that anyone at school particularly liked her. Worst of all, her best friend had left on a mission with her family just one day before we arrived home. The two girls wrote to each other often, talking about how much they missed being together.

Even after many weeks, things got no better. We encouraged our daughter to make more friends and to become more involved in activities at school. We talked to her about the different girls in her seminary class and in our ward, but to no avail. After some time, we determined that what she really needed was a priesthood blessing. We suggested this to her, and in a few days she prepared herself for a blessing and asked for one.

In the blessing, she was told that she would find not only one friend but several. She seemed very encouraged by this, and I'm sure she believed what was said. However, the next few weeks went on in much the same way. No new friends appeared—not even one.

We told her not to lose hope, explaining that the Lord will sometimes try us to see if we will really believe. We reminded her of these words of Moroni:

> I would show unto the world that faith is things which are hoped for and not seen; wherefore, dispute not because ye see not, for ye receive no witness until after the trial of your faith. (Ether 12:6.)

She persisted in faith. Within a few weeks, she began to "pal around" with one of the girls in our ward. Soon they became true friends. Then another friend came on the scene, and then another. Our daughter was happy again, and she learned much from having this new set of friends. In addition, three years later when her old friend returned, within a matter of minutes they were back into their old friendship.

I think my daughter learned a great lesson about the importance of seeking a priesthood blessing when prayer alone doesn't seem to be enough. It showed her how much the Lord loves her, and how he can help with our problems. It surely gave the family an opportunity, after the blessing and with her permission, to pray that she might find friends. Thus, the experience helped all of us increase our faith.

My wife gives another inspiring example of how priesthood blessings can support, comfort, and teach us:

"All my life I have struggled to feel confident in speaking before an audience. I have felt that I didn't have anything of value to offer others; I didn't have anything to say that would particularly help them in their lives. I have struggled with believing that the Lord would speak through me if I were to stand in the very moment to share a testimony or give a talk.

"This has been a special challenge as the wife of a General Authority, since I have the responsibility and obligation to speak in various places along with my husband. To be truthful, this has been somewhat of a cross to bear through the years. I have continually prayed that the Lord would give me confidence to speak by the Spirit, so that the words that needed to be said at that time would really be from my Heavenly Father.

"Not too many years ago I was invited to speak at the Expo on Family Living and Family Values at Brigham Young University. They asked me if I would be the *keynote speaker* at this conference. I couldn't believe, at first, that they really wanted me. My thoughts were, Why would they be asking me? I am not one of these powerful speakers who can share wonderful teachings everywhere they go. I truly felt shocked and surprised at the invitation. But through the years I have always tried to accept my callings. Even though my inclination was to decline, after they reassured me that they really did want me, I did accept.

"At the time we were living in Frankfurt, Germany. I felt somewhat detached from what was going on in the United States, but I had to be prepared to deliver my talk at the time of the next April conference. I prayed that I would be blessed to know what to speak about. Over the course of the next few weeks, I was able to put some thoughts together about how to have the Spirit in our home, how to teach children by the Spirit, and so forth. I felt quite good about the subject, and yet all of the time I had this knot in the pit of my stomach, feeling fear and anxiety over the fact that I was to be the *keynote speaker.* It just petrified me. The more I thought about it the more tied up in knots I became, until I knew I had to do something to alleviate the concern and stress I was having.

"As I pondered my challenge, talked to my husband, and prayed about my feelings, I felt prompted to ask for a priesthood blessing. I felt I had done basically all that I knew how to do in preparing for this assignment. This blessing would help me to know that what I was preparing was the Lord's will, that it was what he wanted me to teach, and that he would help me with my fear and anxiety. Shortly before I received the blessing, the Lord spoke to me with power and clear direction, giving me an added witness that priesthood blessings are truly a wonderful means for the Lord to not only comfort us, but to also teach us lessons in the heart that we will never forget. Blessings are a direct communication from our Heavenly Father to us and confirm that he is close to us.

"As my husband placed his hands on my head and began speaking to me about this assignment, it became clear that the Lord understood my anxieties and my fears. He told me that if I would just trust in him, if I would just leave all my worries, my anxieties, and my fears with him, he would give me the peace that I needed, and that I would be able to speak with confidence and with conviction. The feeling was that I truly would be speaking for him.

"It had been a while since I had felt such confirmation in my heart and mind as when I received this blessing. I was flooded with love for my Heavenly Father, knowing that he did know of my concern and my anxieties. The night before the speaking assignment, at my request my husband gave me another priesthood blessing of reassurance and peace, which again helped me. I was able to sleep without the worry, the fear, and the butterflies in my stomach.

"The next day the talk was presented in a manner that I felt was done with real confidence and conviction. Again I testify of how close the Lord is and how desirous he is to answer our prayers as we seek for instruction and comfort through priesthood blessings."

How the Lord can teach us all through a priesthood blessing!

A priesthood blessing may also be offered to bless your home. Especially during times of contention or difficulties, would it not be wise to bless the home and all who live there? The Lord has told us how to do that in the scriptures (see D&C 75:18–19; Luke 10:5–9); you may also wish to see the guidelines for the dedication of a home given in the current Church handbook of instructions to leaders.

Priesthood blessings will allow you, in a direct way, to better speak, feel, and teach by the Spirit. In the examples I've given, the recipient of the blessing learned valuable lessons from the Lord—and so did everyone else in the family, including the one who pronounced the blessing.

SOME FINAL THOUGHTS

The seven suggestions in this chapter, along with other true principles you may know, will always help bring the Spirit of the Lord as you work with your family or with others. Are these not some of the spiritual gifts that Christ gave to prepare the way for the Holy Ghost to testify and change people's hearts? Give of yourself spiritually, and you will be able to discern the needs of family members and commit them, in the Spirit, to act. Then they will repent and come unto Christ.

You may have children who will not respond to the Master's voice at this time—I repeat, *at this time.* Jesus taught that he could bring people to himself only upon their repentance (see D&C 18:12). But with wayward children and others, we just go on loving them and trying again and again at other times when they may have a more repentant heart and will respond to the Spirit (see 3 Nephi 18:32).

When problems or questions occur in our families, instead of reacting so quickly or giving a pat answer, as some of us do, let us try to humbly turn our hearts to the Lord and to find a way to turn our children's hearts to the Lord. If we will do that, we will have much more success in our families. We can better teach by the Spirit as we have that Spirit more completely with us.

Let us not be discouraged by any of these suggestions. Some might think, "I can't do all of those things. I'm really not able to do them." My answer would be, "Anyone can do these things. We just have to humble ourselves and be believing." And we can start with the ones that are easier for us and then work on using others.

Let us not forget to be vigilant against Satan. He will do all in his power to destroy our understanding of these principles. Let us not discipline when we are angry; true teaching can take place only in a setting where the Spirit of the Lord is present. Then the teaching will be permanently received in the heart of the one who is listening. The single greatest thing a teacher does is provide the environment in which people can have a spiritual experience. How does a teacher do that? These specific spiritual keys will help you provide such an experience. I pray we may all learn how to do it better.

As parents learn to teach with the Spirit, children will learn to hear the voice of the Lord for themselves. They will learn the power of the Spirit through the example of their parents. They will know how to obtain answers to prayer. I bear testimony that if the Lord is humbly invited into a situation, he will be there immediately through the power of the Holy Ghost. Isn't that a great indication of his love?

If parents and children are humble in their hearts, the Spirit of the Lord will come to them immediately. They will feel direction come to them, individually and uniquely. Each will know that the Lord has spoken. That's a great truth that ought not to be overlooked or taken for granted.

I bear testimony that these things are true, and that the Lord will help us as we try to teach our children by the Spirit. If you have any question about teaching by the Spirit, just ask, "What would he do?" If you'll pursue that thought, the Lord will answer the question, and you'll begin to teach more as he did and ultimately become as he is.

May I say again, if you want to know what the Lord would do in a given instance, as you seek to teach by the Spirit, humbly ask him. That isn't just a trite phrase. He will tell you. In other words, you will have been taught by the Spirit as you seek to teach others by the Spirit.

May the Lord bless you and your family. I leave a blessing upon you, in faith, that if you will exercise your righteous desires, prayerfully think about them, ponder them, and work on them, the Lord will lead you step by step along the way, helping you to better learn and teach by the Spirit, until you obtain those spiritual blessings the Lord desires you and your family to have.

Questions to Ponder

1. How can you help your family apply the truths discussed in this chapter?

_____

_____

_____

2. What could you do at home to better teach by the Spirit and have members of your family better receive by the Spirit?

_____

_____

_____

3. Can you take one or more of the principles mentioned in this chapter and find a way to try them out in your family this very week?

_____

_____

_____

4. Are you expressing by word and deed a feeling of pure love for each and every member of your family? How could you increase your manifestations of love for them?

_____

_____

_____

5. Which of your family members may have a real need for a priesthood blessing right now?

_____

_____

_____

CHAPTER 8

THE FRUITS OF THE SPIRIT:
MEASURES OF HOW WE ARE DOING

As we come to the end of this discussion on teaching by the Spirit, I hope you don't become discouraged by the many ideas in this book. We have talked about many different principles that can bless both teacher and student to have the Spirit more strongly. But don't feel that you have to do them all each time you teach. And don't think you have to do everything all at once. I don't believe these ideas need to be approached that way.

I would recommend instead that you prayerfully select a few principles to focus on the next time you teach; then you can try others at other times. Gradually you will become more proficient in different aspects of teaching by the Spirit, and you and those you work with will increasingly be blessed.

I would like to bear testimony of the truthfulness of what is found in these pages. I acknowledge that it is probably impossible for any mortal being to fully describe what it means to teach by the Spirit. I know that I am not fully capable of doing so. But I bear testimony that I have seen the Spirit teach through me and other weak people like me and reach the hearts of men and bring them to the Lord. And I truly believe that the essence of it has to do with the principles and stories we've shared. The bottom line for all of us is believing that the

Lord will really touch others through me and you. I bear testimony that he will.

EXAMPLES OF FRUITS OF THE SPIRIT

Helping Others Turn to the Lord

I also bear witness of some ways we can measure how we're doing as we seek to teach by the Spirit. If we are effectively teaching by the Spirit, for example, we can turn others to the Lord. They can learn to go to him for testimony, instruction, and help. When they do so, both student and teacher have another evidence that the teaching has indeed been done by the Spirit. The very fact that they have turned to the Lord is one of the fruits of the Spirit.

To illustrate that, I'd like to share an experience I had some time ago, where I could see that the teaching of a righteous father and mother had turned their daughter to the Lord.

I had been assigned to visit a particular mission and had arrived at the mission president's home very late, at midnight or even later. The next morning I was scheduled to teach the missionaries and then be on my way out of the country. By the time I prepared to go to bed it was later still, and as I was going downstairs to the bedroom the mission president's wife said, "Elder Cook, you're getting to bed so late, there's no need to get going early in the morning. How about if we have breakfast about eight o'clock or so, which will let you sleep at least a little bit longer."

I said, "Thank you; that will be fine. I'll come upstairs for breakfast about eight o'clock."

Because I was so tired, I was surprised to wake up at about 6:30 A.M. I lay there for a minute, wondering why I had awakened; then a prompting came from the Spirit, "Gene, get up right now and go upstairs. Get up now and go."

I quickly got up, shaved, and got dressed. Upstairs I could hear the family moving about—the mother had told me the night before that she and her husband would teach their children home seminary beginning about 6:00 A.M., and then she would take them to school. After that we would have breakfast.

Within fifteen minutes I made it upstairs, where the mother and her children had gathered at the entryway, coats on, preparing to leave. (The father had already gone to his office in the basement of the house.)

I greeted the three children, a young man who was a returned missionary, a young lady about fifteen, and a twelve-year-old girl whom I'll call Sally. As I shook hands with them I felt a wonderful spirit in them. I told them how much I loved them and shared with them that my children had lived in countries outside the United States as well and indicated that I knew it was difficult and challenging. I sympathized with them about some of the things they were struggling with and asked how they were doing in school and other areas of their lives. We visited five or ten minutes, all of us feeling the power, blessing, and love of the Spirit of the Lord.

After a few minutes the mom said, "Well, we need to be going. Elder Cook, would you be willing to have family prayer with us?" I said "That would be great." So we knelt in the entryway on a rug, and I believe it was the mom who offered a beautiful prayer, asking the Lord to bless her children. Then she took them to school, and I went downstairs to find the husband in his office. We had a chance to have a good visit for about an hour, and then the mother was home and joined us in the office.

She said, "Elder Cook, do you know what happened this morning?"

I said, "No, I'm not sure what you mean."

And she responded, "Well, this morning when Sally got up she came into the kitchen. 'Where's Brother Cook?' she asked. And I said, 'He's still downstairs sleeping because they got in really late last night. He won't be coming up while you're here.' But Sally said, 'Well, doesn't he know that I want to meet him?' And I answered, 'I'm sure he would like to meet you too, but we're not going to wake him up. I'm sorry, but we need to let him sleep.'"

And then this sweet twelve-year-old girl went into her bedroom (by now it was about 6:30 A.M.) and began to pour her heart out to the Lord. "I want to meet Brother Cook," she said. "It's very important to me. Isn't there some way I can meet him?"

Then I told the mother the other side of it, of how I had been awakened at 6:30 A.M. without at first knowing why.

How thankful I am that I followed that prompting. How thankful I am for good parents who taught their young daughter of the power of prayer. And how thankful I am that when we turn to the Lord we can have fruits that bear witness of the presence of the Spirit in our teaching.

THE BURNING FEELINGS OF THE SPIRIT

Another measure that tells us if we are teaching by the Spirit is illustrated in the experience of the two disciples on the road to Emmaus after the death of Christ. As we read in Luke, on the day of the resurrection, before many of the disciples were aware of that great miracle,

> Behold, two of them went that same day to a village called Emmaus. . . . And they talked together of all these things which had happened [i.e., the crucifixion of Christ]. And it came to pass, that, while they communed together and reasoned, Jesus himself drew near, and went with them. But their eyes were holden that they should not know him.
>
> And he said unto them, What manner of communications are these that ye have one to another, as ye walk, and are sad?

And the one of them, whose name was Cleopas, answering said unto him, Art thou only a stranger in Jerusalem, and hast not known the things which are come to pass there in these days?

And he said unto them, What things? And they said unto him, Concerning Jesus of Nazareth, which was a prophet mighty in deed and word before God and all the people: and how the chief priests and our rulers delivered him to be condemned to death, and have crucified him. But we trusted that it had been he which should have redeemed Israel. . . .

Then he said unto them, O fools, and slow of heart to believe all that the prophets have spoken: Ought not Christ to have suffered these things, and to enter into his glory? And beginning at Moses and all the prophets, he expounded unto them in all the scriptures the things concerning himself.

And they drew nigh unto the village, whither they went: and he made as though he would have gone further. But they constrained him, saying, Abide with us: for it is toward evening, and the day is far spent. And he went in to tarry with them.

And it came to pass, as he sat at meat with them, he took bread, and blessed it, and brake, and gave to them. And their eyes were opened, and they knew him; and he vanished out of their sight.

And they said one to another, *Did not our heart burn within us*, while he talked with us by the way, and while he opened to us the scriptures? (Luke 24:13–21, 25–32; emphasis added.)

When these disciples heard the word of Christ, they felt a burning in their hearts as a testimony that they were hearing the truth.

Those we teach can receive the same blessing. When they receive the burning of the Spirit within them, they can know that the Spirit is present and is teaching them. Remember, one of the greatest gifts a teacher can give is to help his "students" to have an experience with the Lord during the teaching. What a wonderful measure the Lord has given to both teacher and student to know that they are speaking and hearing the truth!

SOME ADDITIONAL FRUITS OF THE SPIRIT

There are other ways a teacher can know he or she has taught by the Spirit. And in the same ways, a student can know he or she is receiving by the Spirit. When the Spirit is involved in a teaching situation, you will feel humbled. You will feel peace. You will feel confidence. You will feel repentant. You will feel an increase in your faith, an increase in trust in him, an increase in hope and in love, an increase of light or enlightenment. You will have an increased desire to do what you've learned. You will feel uplifted. You will feel the truth. You will have a desire to share. And lastly, you will have a resolve that "I will go and do."

The scriptures testify plainly of the fruits of having the Spirit with us, which are also the fruits of teaching and learning by the Spirit. One passage that is very helpful in this regard is Alma 58:10 (which, in my opinion, is one of the best scriptures in the entire Book of Mormon on the *way* prayer works):

"Therefore we did pour out our souls in prayer to God . . . "

What did they do? They poured out their souls. They didn't just casually say their prayers. They *poured out their souls* to God. Have you as teachers done that for one of your students who is really struggling? Have you poured out your soul or even fasted for him or her? Your students may never know it, but you may be an instrument in bringing them to Christ. Have you done this for your children, or perhaps for people you work with as a leader?

I'm impressed with the next line:

" . . . that he would strengthen us and deliver us . . . "

Isn't that what we're usually praying for? Other than giving thanks, we're usually asking to be strengthened or delivered from some problem. It's a pretty good description of the purpose of most of our prayers. Then, in verse 11, we learn how the Lord answers a petition to the heavens:

"Yea, and it came to pass that the Lord our God did visit us with assurances that he would deliver us . . . "

Assurances, evidence the Spirit of the Lord is there. This doesn't necessarily sound like a big thing—and yet it is a big thing, isn't it? The Lord sends us confidence and assurance that we can go forward.

" . . . yea, insomuch that he did speak peace to our souls . . . "

This is the second blessing he will give us as answer to our prayers.

" . . . and did grant unto us great faith . . . "

This is a third blessing he sends.

" . . . and did cause us that we should hope for our deliverance in him . . . "

The fourth blessing is a blessing of hope. Those four blessings—*assurance, peace, faith,* and *hope*—are fruits of the Spirit. They **are evidences** that the Lord is present. These are what he breathes into us so we can then go and do what has to be done to accomplish his purposes.

Then verse 12 indicates what happens when those gifts are breathed into you by the Lord:

"And we did take courage . . . "

Courage tells us "I think that I can do this," or "I think I know what to do." Courage comes when the heavens have been opened.

"And we did take courage with our small force which we had received, and were fixed with a determination to conquer."

The Lord can breathe that resolve into us, that fixed determination to conquer, and when that happens, you have really been given an answer to prayer.

These fruits of the Spirit come with heartfelt prayer; they also come when we teach and learn by the Spirit. When our students (be they in a Church class, in a family, or in a ward council meeting) feel *assurance, peace, faith, hope,* and *courage,* both they and we can know that the Spirit has been present in the teaching we have tried to do.

Here are a number of other fruits of the Spirit, as revealed by the scriptures. When we experience these fruits in our teaching and learning, we can thereby know that the Spirit is indeed present.

The Fruits of Revelation and of Teaching with Power and Authority

Alma did rejoice exceedingly to see his brethren; and what added more to his joy, they were still his brethren in the Lord; yea, and they had waxed strong in the knowledge of the truth; for they were men of a sound understanding and they had searched the scriptures diligently, that they might know the word of God.

But this is not all; they had given themselves to much prayer, and fasting; therefore they had the spirit of prophecy, and the spirit of revelation, and when they taught, they taught with power and authority of God. (Alma 17:2–3; see also Mosiah 18:26; Helaman 5:18; 3 Nephi 7:16–18; D&C 28:3.)

The Fruits of Joy, Peace, Hope, and Love

Now the God of hope fill you with all joy and peace in believing, that ye may abound in hope, through the power of the Holy Ghost. (Romans 15:13.)

But the fruit of the Spirit is love, joy, peace, longsuffering, gentleness, goodness, faith, meekness, temperance. (Galatians 5:22–23.)

The Fruit of Peace

Did I not speak peace to your mind concerning the matter? What greater witness can you have than from God? (D&C 6:23.)

The Fruits of Enlightenment and Joy

Verily, verily, I say unto you, I will impart unto you of my Spirit, which shall enlighten your mind, which shall fill your soul with joy. (D&C 11:13.)

The Fruit of Repentance

And it came to pass that they did preach with great power, insomuch that they did confound many of those dissenters who had gone over from the Nephites, insomuch that they came forth and did confess their sins and were baptized unto repentance, and immediately returned to the Nephites to endeavor to repair unto them the wrongs which they had done. (Helaman 5:17.)

The Fruit of Action or Obedience

Now after Alma had spoken these words, they sent forth unto him desiring to know whether they should believe in one God, that they might obtain this fruit of which he had spoken, or how they should plant the seed, or the word of which he had spoken, which he said must be planted in their hearts; or in what manner they should begin to exercise their faith. (Alma 33:1.)

When these fruits appear in the lives of students, we can know that the teacher is teaching by the Spirit of the Lord and the students are receiving by the same Spirit, because these are the fruits that come forth when the Spirit is present. What blessings these are from a gracious Heavenly Father!

TEACHINGS THAT BEAR FRUIT OVER TIME

Sometimes our teaching doesn't bear fruit immediately—but if we truly seek to teach by the Spirit, the seed will be planted, and the fruit may grow when the circumstance requires, or when the person is ready.

One evening some years ago I decided to take two of my sons to a movie. We usually go as a family, but I decided to surprise them and take just the two of them. We took off for a nearby theater to see a show that we had been told was a good movie, and we went anticipating a fun time.

After the first few minutes in the theater it was evident that there was going to be a lot of very bad language in the movie. I asked the boys a couple of times, "What do you think we should do?"—perhaps more in the spirit of seeing where they were in their thinking than anything else. (To be honest, in the beginning I was really enjoying the show.) But the language became even worse, and finally one of my sons said, "Dad, I don't think it's right that we should stay here." His brother quickly agreed. They both sat there staring at Dad to see what he would say.

Finally I said, "Well, I think you're right. Let's go." So with some reluctance—and yet knowing we were doing the right thing—we walked out of the movie within fifteen minutes after it had started.

We ended up going somewhere else and doing something fun together. I have since thought of that as a good example of how our teaching can bear fruit days or weeks or even years later. I wasn't teaching my sons at that moment about the evils of swearing or of bad movies. But my wife and I had taught them such things more than once in the past, and they remembered and applied the teachings on that day in that theater. Their action that day blessed not only them but also their father.

Sometimes the seed of learning lies dormant for many years, only to sprout and grow and bear fruit when the person finally allows it to do so. Here is an impressive account told by a sister who left the Church but who came back when the fruits of the Spirit began to take hold in her life:

"I had been excommunicated from The Church of Jesus Christ of Latter-day Saints for six years—six years with a lifestyle of partying and drinking with my friends. I figured that was the best way to get through the rough trials of my life—to drown my heartaches in alcohol and parties.

"One night we gathered around the bar and ordered our drinks. I laughed a lot and listened to everyone tell of their drunken immoral behavior. Then a new thought popped into my head. Where had it come from? All of a sudden I began to analyze the friends I was with. None of them had any rules and lived only for today. I suddenly remembered a Book of Mormon scripture:

"'Yea, and there shall be many which shall say: Eat, drink, and be merry, for tomorrow we die; and it shall be well with us. And there shall also be many which shall say: Eat, drink, and be merry; nevertheless, fear God—he will justify in committing a little sin; . . . and at last we shall be saved in the kingdom of God.' (2 Nephi 28:7–8.)

"I looked around the bar and at all the laughing people and suddenly recognized who they were: These were the people in the great and spacious building in Lehi's dream! (See 1 Nephi 8:33; 12:18.) It hit me with so much power that it nearly took my breath away! Then the next thought penetrated my mind with deep emotion. What was I doing alongside these people?

"I had learned about Lehi's dream sometime in seminary. Now with a power that penetrated my heart, I saw myself in that building with these terrible sinners, mocking Jesus Christ. At the same time, the Lord was whispering truths to me. I looked at the people in the bar and imagined they were all mocking and pointing their fingers at me.

"A window nearby caught my attention and as I gazed through it I saw myself in the big and spacious building pointing my own finger and laughing at my family. They were holding on to the rod of iron, taking turns partaking of the fruit. They saw me watching them and began to call out to me: 'Come here and take hold of the rod of iron and taste of the fruit.' But much like Laman and Lemuel, I would not. Great wells of tears filled my eyes and I began to visibly weep.

"I excused myself and found a bathroom where I could get my thoughts together. I took a deep breath and went back out to my friends and tried to laugh the whole thing off. But the vision returned, this time with even more forcefulness. The whisperings of the Spirit were very powerful and real. I knew in my heart that God had spoken to me. I had heard his very voice audibly call me by name, telling me to join my family at the rod of iron. I actually heard him call my name three different times. I could not deny it, but I also could not explain this to my friends. I told them that I had to leave and go home, and that is just what I did.

"Later, as I began to read the Book of Mormon again, I stumbled on a scripture that had a very profound effect on my decision to return to Christ and repent of my sins:

"'And now it shall come to pass, that whosoever shall not take upon him the name of Christ must be called by some other name; . . . I would that ye should remember to retain the name written always in your hearts, that ye are not found on the left hand of God, but that ye hear and know the voice by which ye shall be called, and also, the name by which he shall call you.

"'For how knoweth a man the master whom he has not served, and who is a stranger unto him, and is far from the thoughts and intents of his heart? . . .

"'Therefore, I would that ye should be steadfast and immovable, always abounding in good works, that Christ, the Lord God Omnipotent, may seal you his.' (Mosiah 5:10, 12–13, 15.)

"I felt the power of the love of God for me manifested in my heart. For the past six years, I had not so much as given him a thought or acknowledged him in prayer. He had been a stranger to me because I would not open the door to him. That thought and this scripture brought me to my knees. I began to beg for forgiveness and mercy from the Lord. I could not run from God any longer, nor could I continue to deny him. I knew I had a very long road to climb. I knew that time was running out, and that I must make a stand for what I knew to be true.

"I now was filled with the strength to endure what was ahead of me, because I knew my Savior cared enough to leave his flock and come looking for me, a rebellious, runaway sinner. This testimony of the Lord's great love for me has filled my life to overflowing. I will forever remember that night when the Lord came looking for me, picked me up, and wrapped me in his arms of love and mercy, rescuing me from myself in an evil world."

This sister continues her story, telling about her experience in being rebaptized. After a disciplinary council where she was approved for rebaptism, and while awaiting her baptism, she writes:

"The next month was full of anxiety—and thanksgiving for this incomprehensible blessing that was about to unfold before me. I desperately wanted to go down into the waters of baptism and shed the evil person of the past and become born again. I yearned to have my name re-entered in the records of the Church, to be counted worthy to have my name written in the Book of Life as a true and faithful member of The Church of Jesus Christ of Latter-day Saints. Never in my life had I struggled so hard to endure the test of time.

"Finally, the great day arrived. I was dressed all in white. My youngest brother baptized me by immersion. As I came up out of the water I was filled with the power of the Holy Ghost.

My chest felt as if it would burst and my throat and eyes were choking with tears of joy. Soaking wet, I ran into the women's dressing room, where I wept uncontrollably. Only the Lord and I will ever know of the great love and joy that was shared between us on that sweet and peaceful November day. He witnessed to me that I was a new person, completely forgiven of all my sins.

"My past was gone, and all my sins were washed away. I felt the Atonement come alive in my life! I felt the Lord's loving grace and mercy change my heart and fill my soul with peace and love. It was astonishing to me!

"When I was confirmed a member of the Church by another brother, I felt the impression that the spiritual hands of my deceased father were placed on my head along with the other priesthood brethren. Oh, what a joyful day it was! Family and friends surrounded me, sharing the wonderful spirit that permeated every heart . . . witnessing the miraculous return of a lost sheep found and brought back into the arms of the Master Shepherd.

"How marvelous the atonement of Jesus Christ! He can change a heart and turn a life completely around, if only we are *willing* to repent and turn to him with full purpose of heart. I will forever be thankful for his great love and mercy that was shown me on that most sacred day."

Consider the sweet power of this testimony. Seeds of truth had been planted in this sister's heart years earlier, seeds from her parents and family, from seminary, from many Sundays at church. But they lay dormant within her, bearing no fruit. Then, in the Lord's love and mercy, he reached out to her—and even in a moment of transgression she heard his voice! She had been taught by the Spirit and, when she was willing, the fruits of the Spirit came into her life.

THE FAR-REACHING POWER OF THE SPIRIT

We've talked about how men and women stand before the Saints to teach by the Spirit, how parents teach children and children teach parents by the Spirit, how we can teach by the Spirit as leaders and home teachers and visiting teachers. Now here is one final story of how the Lord lovingly reaches out directly with his Spirit to touch the lives of his children—and in the process teaches and blesses many. The Lord is so powerful and so loving that sometimes he will touch and inspire and influence someone through his Spirit without them even knowing it.

To illustrate how effectively, and yet subtly, the Lord can reach his children through his Spirit, I would like to share an experience my family was blessed with. This experience demonstrates that sometimes the Lord's teaching is so subtle that if you're not really watching you may not even know you've been taught.

One Christmas season not too long ago we had a son serving his mission in Brazil. At the time, my wife and I, with our younger children, were serving in Europe. Just a day or two before Christmas, my wife had been blessed to serve a special dinner to all the missionaries in the Germany Frankfurt Mission. About one hundred of them came to eat, most all of them very hungry and with big appetites. As each one came down the food line, my wife said, "I just delighted in loading up their plates." She filled them so full that they almost dripped over the side.

When she came home and began to talk about the dinner, I could tell that she had had a significant emotional and spiritual experience. Some people would say that all she had done was "just feed the missionaries." But I could see that something more had happened that day.

I said, "Honey, you've been around thousands of missionaries for many years. Why did this particular experience touch you so deeply?"

And she said, "Well, while I was loading the plates and doing my best to feed all those young men and women, I prayed over and over again that someone would remember our son in Brazil. Because of the particular area he's in, I knew his chances would be very slim to have dinner with anybody. But I just prayed that some other mother would remember my boy. And I prayed that the Lord wouldn't forget my son, so that somehow he would have a nice Christmas dinner."

As you know, missionaries are allowed to call home on Christmas Day. Our son was not able to call us until a few days later. When he finally did, this is what he told us.

"On Christmas Day we went out to make our phone calls home. My companion finally got through to his parents, and I sat and listened for about an hour as he talked to his family. My heart just ached, because I wanted to talk to my own family— but we could not get a call through to Germany. After repeated tries I finally gave up.

"We had no dinner invitation, and we decided that since it was Christmas Day, we would eat out at a restaurant, which we seldom do. We pooled our money and found that all we had was six dollars between us. We knew that would never buy a Christmas dinner, but we decided to go to an inexpensive restaurant and order something cheap."

But the only restaurant they could find open was a fairly expensive place. So they agreed, "We'll go in and we'll just order some pizza, and that will be our Christmas dinner." But when they got inside and looked at the menu, they were disappointed to see that even pizza was more than six dollars. They didn't know what to do. As they stood there trying to decide, they saw the people at the salad bar, weighing their salads. They said to each other, "We'll just go up and make two salads, and we'll weigh them to the maximum amount of what the three dollars will cover."

As they were beginning to get their plates, an older women came up and tapped my son's companion on the shoulder. She said to him in Portuguese, "Young man, why would I have the strongest impression that I should buy you two young men dinner?"

They said, "Oh no, you couldn't do that."

And she said, "Yes, you take this menu and pick whatever dinner you want. I am paying for your entire dinner."

They said, "Are you a member of our church?"

"No, I'm not," she said, looking at their name tags. And then she told them she was a member of another church that had given our church some very difficult times in that particular city. In fact, just a few weeks earlier, some members of that church had invited three Protestant ministers over to lie in wait for these two young missionaries—and she had been part of that.

Our son said, "Before I met this lady, my feelings about her church had really been negative, but there in the restaurant, all of the sudden they were washed clean. I saw that the members of that church were well-intentioned and were just trying to do what they thought the Lord would want."

Because of the generosity of this lady, who was touched by the Lord, perhaps without even knowing it, they had a wonderful Christmas dinner. "As my companion and I walked out into the street, fully satisfied with a great Christmas dinner," my son said, "we both seemed to hear the Lord say, 'Merry Christmas, my sons. You're my missionaries.'"

As you can imagine, after our son related that special experience, it was my wife's turn to tell him about the prayer she had offered for her son many thousands of miles away just a few days earlier.

SEEKING TO TEACH LIKE THE MASTER TEACHER

I am constantly impressed at how the Lord is able to do things in such a majestic way. He can teach a missionary of his love and concern on a special day; he teaches a nonmember lady who followed a prompting; he teaches a General Authority and his wife and family; and he teaches you by sharing that story.

The Lord's ways are so marvelous. He teaches all of us freely by his Spirit, if we will listen. Through his Spirit, he prompts someone to pray for something. Then he prompts others, who may not even be members of the Church, to respond. In this experience of my wife and my son, we can see how the Lord teaches and reaches by the Spirit—and can do so even without using mortal teachers to help.

But mortal teachers are a key part of his plan. He will often speak to others through us. And I hope and pray that as you set aside this book, you will do so with a determination to be more committed. I pray that we will try harder to humble our hearts more, to be more believing, to truly pray to the Lord that he might use us as instruments in his hands to reach his children and to bring them to the Lord.

I bear testimony that the Lord does indeed want us to teach by his Spirit, and I pray that the Lord will bless each of us to be more effective in doing so. I pray that we will go to him and learn from him how to do it. As we do we will teach with a greater power and authority than we have ever known before. We will be able to reach people in ways we have not been able to reach them before. We will be able to help others turn more fully to Christ. And we will find ourselves turning more fully to Christ, as we learn to rely upon him and to teach as he, the great Master Teacher, did.

May the Lord bless each of us to grow to be better at

teaching by the Spirit, which blessing I also seek in the name of Jesus Christ.

QUESTIONS TO PONDER

1. What type of spiritual measurements can we use to tell us how we are doing in listening or teaching by the Spirit?

_____

_____

_____

2. Sometimes the evidence that someone has been taught by the Spirit does not come until years later. But how can the teacher know at the very time that the Spirit has assisted in the teaching?

_____

_____

_____

3. What do you need to do personally to be more observant and thus better recognize the fruits of the Spirit?

_____

_____

_____

INDEX

Action, as a fruit of the Spirit, 203

Analogies, Christ's use of, 25

Application, of truths: in teaching, 64–65; learner's responsibility for, 153–57; experience regarding, with German family, 154–57

Assurance, as a fruit of the Spirit, 200–202

Attitude, a believing, 151–53, 191–92

Ballard, M. Russell, on teaching the family, 159

Behavior, changing, 170

Believing attitude, a: as a prerequisite to learning, 151–53; Harold B. Lee on, 153; in teaching the family, 191–92

Benson, Ezra Taft, on seeking priesthood blessings, 127–28

Blessings, priesthood. *See* Priesthood blessings

Burning of the Spirit, 198–200

Caldwell, C. Max, on preparing to teach, 79

Church Handbook of Instructions, Book 2: Priesthood and Auxiliary Leaders, 3

Classes, role of learners in: story of Gospel Doctrine class and, 143–45; student's responsibility in, 144–45

Cook, Elsie Hanna, 4–6

Courage, as a fruit of the Spirit, 200–202

Doctrine: teaching true, 52–53; knowing what to teach, 53–54; limitations on teaching, 54–55; Boyd K. Packer on changing behavior through, 170

Dress standards, using scriptures to teach, 167–70

Ears, opening one's: Marion G. Romney on hearing, 145; listening vs. hearing, 145–46;

215